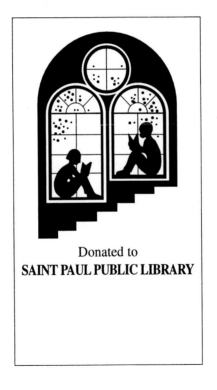

The Warren Court and
the Pursuit of Justice

Also by Morton J. Horwitz

Transformation of American Law, 1780–1860

Transformation of American Law, 1870–1960:
The Crisis of Legal Orthodoxy

American Legal Realism
(with William W. Fisher and Thomas Reed, eds.)

MORTON J. HORWITZ

The Warren Court and the Pursuit of Justice

A CRITICAL ISSUE

HILL AND WANG

A division of Farrar, Straus and Giroux

New York

Hill and Wang
A division of Farrar, Straus and Giroux
19 Union Square West, New York 10003

For Jennifer, Lauren, and Karen

Acknowledgments

My desire to write a book on the Warren Court has been fueled and sustained by my students, especially the bright and enthusiastic Harvard undergraduates who have enrolled in my college course on the Warren Court, Historical Study B-61. They have flocked to this course in search of authentic beacons of political enlightenment—historical illustrations through which they might still experience a time when American idealism showed its most generous and hopeful face.

My thanks to Harvard Law student Danielle M. Spinelli, an outstanding research assistant and an exceptional editor, and to Lauren Horwitz, who helped to create a fine index.

My deepest thanks to Pnina Lahav, who first suggested this project and has supported and encouraged me throughout. I am also grateful for her review of the manuscript.

Contents

A Note to the Reader

My book is addressed to the person who wishes to acquire some introductory knowledge of the historical significance of the Supreme Court without being distracted or intimidated by legal technicalities. I wish to show the general reader how interesting and exciting the intense study of a particular, focused historical era of the Supreme Court can be. The Warren Court is certainly a dramatic example of the relationship between constitutional law and history.

When Earl Warren became Chief Justice in 1953, few would have predicted that when he retired sixteen years later the Warren Court would be remembered for inaugurating a progressive constitutional revolution that changed the entire landscape of American law and life. At the time, few believed that the Supreme Court was institutionally capable of initiating fundamental constitutional change. For most of American history, in fact, the Court had thrown the weight of its authority behind the owners of property, whether of slave, corporate, or landed property. After the Civil War, for complex reasons, the Court systematically interpreted the Civil War Amendments—the Thirteenth through Fifteenth Amendments—to deprive newly freed slaves and their descendants of virtually all the protections that the proponents of the Amendments hoped had been conferred.

The Warren Court was thus the first to attempt to redeem the promises of the Civil War Amendments for black citizens. Coming right at the beginning of the Warren Era, the historic decision in *Brown* v. *Board of Education* was a nuclear event in American constitutional law that generated multiple tidal waves of reactions that ricocheted back upon the Court. These ranged from Southern white "massive resistance" against desegregation to an inspired and inspiring civil rights movement that triggered novel questions about constitutional protections of social protest movements.

As Earl Warren was about to become Chief Justice, the Supreme Court, in the midst of that Cold War–inspired anti-Communist paranoia known as McCarthyism, had upheld a series of major assaults on civil liberties that were justified in terms of national security. Despite the eloquent free-speech dissents of Holmes and Brandeis during the 1920s, the Supreme Court continued to resist most efforts to expand freedom of speech. One of the most significant achievements of the Warren Court was not only its gradual dismantling of McCarthyism in American law and life but also its dramatic incorporation of the Holmes-Brandeis vision of free speech into the Court's interpretation of the First Amendment.

The Warren Court's civil rights and civil liberties decisions thoroughly transformed American constitutional law. For the first time in American history, the Supreme Court demonstrated its concern and support for the weak and the powerless, the marginal and the socially scorned. It paid new attention to, in Justice Brennan's words, "the essential dignity and worth of each individual."

Through this process, the Warren Court also dramatically reconstituted the map of American political theory. For the first time, democracy became the foundational value in American constitutional discourse, encouraging the Warren Court to redefine the relationship between judicial review and democracy. In the end, the Court managed to transcend the traditionally dichotomous treatment of judicial review and democracy as well as of liberty and equality.

Ultimately, the test of the historical significance of the Warren Court is whether it managed to leave a lasting legacy of progressive interpretations of the Constitution, interpretations that, even when subsequently overturned, continue to inspire future generations of judges, lawyers, and students.

—M.J.H.

The Warren Court and
the Pursuit of Justice

I

Constituting the Warren Court

This book seeks to capture one of the most eventful and influential periods in the history of the United States Supreme Court—the sixteen years between 1953 and 1969 during which Earl Warren served as Chief Justice. From the perspective of more than a quarter century later, the Warren Court is increasingly recognized as having initiated a unique and revolutionary chapter in American constitutional history. Beginning with its first major decision declaring racial segregation unconstitutional in *Brown* v. *Board of Education* (1954), the Court regularly handed down opinions that have transformed American constitutional doctrine and, in turn, profoundly affected American society.

The range of the Warren Court's influence has been enormous. The Court initiated a revolution in race relations; expanded the constitutional guarantee of "equal protection of the laws"; dramatically expanded the protections of freedom of speech and press; overturned unequally apportioned legislative districts; accorded defendants in criminal cases massively expanded constitutional protections; and recognized for the first time a constitutional right to privacy.

Before we can understand the Warren Court revolution, it is necessary to realize that when we break into the flow of history in order to focus intensively on a particular period, we may underestimate the importance of events that preceded and followed our own specific period. So, for example, we should not assume that *Brown* v. *Board of Education* came out of nowhere. Rather, the stage was already set for *Brown* by earlier struggles over racial segregation.

Just as important, while it is convenient to terminate our study of the Warren Court in 1969, when Chief Justice Warren resigned, we should not be misled into thinking that the influence of the Warren Court ended the day Earl Warren retired. Two of the most famous post–Warren Court decisions, for example, were deeply influenced by constitutional changes initiated earlier by the Warren Court. *Roe* v. *Wade* (1973), establishing a woman's constitutional right to an abortion, and *Furman* v. *Georgia* (1972), declaring existing capital punishment laws unconstitutional, were handed down after the Warren Court had formally come to a close. Similarly, the first case extending the Constitution to bar gender discrimination, *Reed* v. *Reed* (1971), was decided only after the Warren Court had passed into history. Yet the path had been prepared by Warren Court decisions expanding the scope of the Equal Protection Clause of the Fourteenth Amendment. As long as we bear in mind that any effort to study a particular period may unconsciously understate what went before or came after, the benefits to be derived from an intensive historical focus seem clearly worth it.

The Justices of the Warren Court

The Warren Court is not just an abstraction. It consisted of individual justices—who constitute an extraordinarily able and interesting group—with different backgrounds and different viewpoints about law and life. We need to focus first on the justices who made up the liberal majority that produced the Warren Court revolution.

When Earl Warren was appointed Chief Justice by President Eisenhower in 1953, only two of the justices who would eventually constitute the future liberal majority were already on the bench. First was Hugo L. Black of Alabama, a New Deal stalwart in the United States Senate, who, in 1937, became President Franklin Delano Roosevelt's first appointment to the Court. Before being elected to the Senate, he had served as a part-time police court judge and county prosecuting attorney.

Shortly after his nomination to the Court had been confirmed by the Senate, it was revealed that Black had once been a member of the racist Ku Klux Klan in Alabama. He explained that he had remained a member for only two years and had long since resigned. Indeed, it may have been impossible to be elected in Alabama without Klan membership. As we shall see, Black repudiated this part of his heritage and was one of the first justices strongly to support the view that the Court needed to overrule its earlier decisions legitimating racial segregation.

Black was raised in a Southern evangelical Baptist family. His religious background is crucial in understanding his strong reading of the First Amendment as requiring a "wall of separation" between church and state, and also his extremely doctrinaire views on how to interpret the text of the Constitution. "[The] Constitution is my legal bible," he once proclaimed; "its plan of our government is my plan and its destiny my destiny. I cherish every word of it, from the first to the last, and I personally deplore even the slightest deviation from its least important commands." Black always carried a copy of the Constitution in his jacket pocket, perhaps imitating the manner in which his evangelical forebears regularly carried copies of the Bible.

The other liberal justice already on the Court when Warren became Chief Justice was William O. Douglas, one of the most brilliant and irascible figures ever to sit on the Court. Appointed at the age of forty-one in 1939 by President Roosevelt, Douglas was the second youngest person ever named to the Court. He retired after serving longer (thirty-six years) than any other Justice, breaking Black's record of thirty-four years.

Douglas was appointed after a significant career in government. A professor at Yale Law School and a leading figure in the movement for legal reform known as Legal Realism, Douglas served as a member and then chairman of the Securities and Exchange Commission, which had been created by the New Deal to regulate trading on the nation's stock markets. Just before he was appointed to the Court, he had been chosen to be dean of Yale Law School.

Douglas's childhood background seems to have had a lasting influence on his views of law and life. Shortly after his family moved to Yakima, Washington, where he grew up, Douglas's father, a Protestant minister, died, plunging the family into dire poverty when Douglas was only five years old. His great autobiography, *Go East, Young Man*, tells the story of his youthful struggles against poverty and poor health. Having contracted polio as a boy, in order to strengthen his body he began mountain climbing, which became a lifelong passion. His love of nature combined with his deep feelings of being a "loner" to produce an intense and brooding personality. From an early age, he explained in his autobiography, he strongly identified with outsiders, even to the extent of joining hoboes who slipped into railroad boxcars for trips across the country. This empathy for the poor and the socially scorned not only marked Douglas's legal worldview but also was to become a strong feature of the jurisprudence of the Warren Court.

Like Douglas, Earl Warren grew up in a poor family. He was born in Los Angeles, the son of a Norwegian immigrant who earned $70 a month as a repairman for the Southern Pacific Railroad before losing his job when he joined a union. (Later, after Warren had become a lawyer, his father was murdered; the murder was never solved.) Warren himself worked on the railroads in his early years, experiencing at first hand the inequality of power between large corporations and vulnerable and unorganized workers.

Warren worked his way through college and law school. After a brief period in private practice, he began a half century of public service. Starting as a deputy in the Alameda County district attorney's office, he then served for thirteen years as a crusading district attorney and four years as California's attorney general; he had begun his third term as a progressive Republican governor of California when he was appointed to the Court. In 1948, he ran for Vice President on the unsuccessful Republican ticket headed by Thomas Dewey.

Earl Warren was a commanding figure. When Eisenhower appointed him Chief Justice, Warren was such a popular governor that when running for his second term, he had been nominated by both Democrats and Republicans. In a deal made at the 1952 Republican Convention, Warren ended his own presidential aspirations and threw his votes to Eisenhower, who promised, if elected President, to nominate Warren to the first open seat on the Supreme Court. On the basis of that promise, Warren had decided to resign from the California governorship to accept Eisenhower's offer to become Solicitor General, the government's chief advocate before the Supreme Court. Only someone as conscientious—and as personally secure—as Warren would even have entertained a move to the Solicitor Generalship, a position of much lower status. But he apparently understood that his years in politics had left him unprepared for the intellectually high-powered atmosphere of the Supreme Court. Nobody had anticipated that Chief Justice Fred M. Vinson would die of a heart attack before Warren could assume the Solicitor Generalship, leaving the Chief Justice's seat open. The Eisenhower Administration tried briefly to deny that Eisenhower's promise had included the Chief Justiceship, but Warren prevailed on the President to honor his promise. Warren's unexpectedly sudden elevation to Chief Justice deprived him of the learning experience that the Solicitor Generalship would have provided; it also explains why it took Warren several years before he actually found his own direction on the Court.

Three years after Warren became Chief Justice, the future liberal majority was further augmented when President Eisenhower appointed an obscure New Jersey Supreme Court justice,

William J. Brennan, Jr., to the Court. An Irish Catholic Democrat, Brennan happened to be an almost random beneficiary of a reelection strategy by which the Eisenhower Administration sought to retain the support of the large number of Catholic Democrats who had voted for Eisenhower in his first presidential election.

Brennan, who was to become the most important intellectual influence on the Warren Court, would also rank as one of the greatest justices in the nation's history. Given the impressive brainpower of so many of Brennan's colleagues—Frankfurter, Black, Douglas, Harlan, and Fortas possessed unusually powerful intellects—it was no small achievement for Brennan to attain such preeminence. What is even more remarkable is that there is little in Brennan's biography that prepares us for his astonishing performance as a justice, one that continued until 1990—for twenty-one additional years after the Warren Court had ended.

The second of eight children born to parents who had immigrated to the United States in the 1890s, Brennan grew up in Newark, New Jersey. His father, by Brennan's own account the most influential person in his life, moved up from shoveling coal in a local brewery to become a prominent labor leader and municipal official. One of Brennan's most dramatic childhood memories was seeing his father carried home from a union picket line, bloodied and beaten by police.

An honors graduate of the Wharton School of the University of Pennsylvania and a high-ranking graduate of Harvard Law School, Brennan returned to New Jersey to practice law with a prominent firm in the 1930s. After serving in the Army during World War II, he returned to private practice after the war, where he became a leader of the New Jersey court reform movement. He was appointed to the state's trial court in 1949 and, within a three-year period, progressed through the judicial hierarchy to the state supreme court, where he served for four years before being elevated to the United States Supreme Court.

There are a few clues in Brennan's pre-Court legal career to the path that the future justice would pursue. Several of his New Jersey Supreme Court decisions expanded the rights of criminal defendants, one of the clear themes of the Warren Court. During his tenure on the New Jersey Supreme Court, which coincided with the height of McCarthyite frenzy, Brennan also risked his future judicial advancement by making speeches that provocatively alluded to McCarthy's abuse of the congressional investigative powers, using words like "Salem witch-hunts" and "inquisition." Senator McCarthy made these speeches a major issue at Brennan's confirmation hearings, and was the only senator to vote against his confirmation.

A source of inspiration for Brennan that may have been overlooked was his Roman Catholicism, which also played a major part in his nomination. No Catholic had been appointed to the Court since Justice Frank Murphy's death seven years earlier, and Eisenhower had promised the conservative clergyman and powerful Church figure Francis Cardinal Spellman to appoint a Catholic to the next vacant seat. In fact, before announcing Brennan's nomination, an Eisenhower aide contacted Brennan's parish priest to verify that he attended Sunday Mass regularly. Brennan's appointment did not, however, satisfy Spellman, who was angry that Eisenhower had chosen someone he did not consider a "proper, practicing Catholic." And in fact Brennan's decisions on the Court owed little or nothing to conservative Church dogma.

Brennan recognized that, in some cases, his beliefs as a Catholic might conflict with what the Constitution requires; he left no doubt that in his mind, his Catholicism took second place to his obligation to the Constitution. In his confirmation hearings, Brennan emphasized that his only allegiance as a justice would be to the Constitution. And in an interview much later, he said, "As a Roman Catholic I might do as a private citizen what a Roman Catholic does, and that is one thing, but to the extent that that conflicts with what I think the Constitution means and requires, then my religious beliefs have to give way."

When asked to name the most difficult decision he had made as a justice, Brennan responded, "[T]he school prayer cases . . . In the face of my whole lifelong experience as a Roman Catholic, to say that prayer was not an appropriate thing in public schools, that gave me quite a hard time. I struggled." Brennan referred to *Engel* v. *Vitale* (1962) and *Abington School District* v. *Schempp* (1963), in which the Court held that the First Amendment's Establishment Clause ("Congress shall make no law respecting an establishment of religion") forbade school prayer. *Engel* and *Schempp* were the most far-reaching extension of Justice Black's idea that the First Amendment required a "wall of separation" between church and state. The decisions aroused widespread indignation; Cardinal Spellman said of *Engel* that it struck "at the very heart of the Godly tradition in which America's children had so long been raised." Whether or not the school prayer decisions required Brennan to elevate the Constitution over the Church, as he suggested, the decisions must have confirmed Spellman's worst fears about his appointment.

Brennan's agreement with the majority in the abortion case, *Roe* v. *Wade* (1973), a decision widely denounced by the Church hierarchy, might be another instance in which his Catholicism "gave way" to the Constitution. It may also be, however, that Brennan was influenced by the liberal strand of Catholicism that came to the fore during the 1960s. Pope John XXIII convened Vatican II in Rome between 1962 and 1965, substantially reforming many of the Church's teachings. For many American Catholic liberals, Vatican II was a powerful source of affirmation; its effect on Brennan deserves further investigation.

While Black, Douglas, Warren, and Brennan formed a solid liberal wing and were able to influence many decisions, it took nine years before the Warren Court's liberal majority was finally consolidated, when in 1962 President John F. Kennedy named Arthur J. Goldberg to replace the retiring leader of the Court's conservative bloc, Justice Felix Frankfurter. Until becoming Kennedy's Secretary of Labor, Goldberg had served his entire career as a labor lawyer, becoming general counsel in 1948 to the once quite radical labor union the United Steelworkers (CIO). A child of Russian immigrants, he was appointed to the Court's so-called Jewish seat, which had been occupied before Frankfurter by Justice Benjamin N. Cardozo. President Johnson persuaded Goldberg to leave the Court in 1965 to become United States Permanent Representative to the United Nations, a position Goldberg wrongly believed would be a stepping-stone to the Vice Presidency. Johnson named another child of Jewish immigrants, Abe Fortas, to replace Goldberg.

Fortas had had a long-standing political connection to Johnson. As Johnson's lawyer, he successfully fought off a challenge to Johnson's questionable eighty-seven-vote primary election victory margin that eventually sent him, in 1948, to the United States Senate from Texas with the nickname "Landslide Lyndon." When he was a young man, Fortas's career was also substantially enhanced by his service in Washington for William O. Douglas, who had been his professor at Yale Law School and whose reformist Legal Realism was a major influence on Fortas. Fortas eventually became a founding partner of the prestigious Washington law firm Arnold, Fortas & Porter. When he was practicing law, two of his most important public interest cases involved successful arguments for reform of the insanity defense in *Durham* v. *U.S.* (1954) and for a constitutional right to counsel in state criminal cases in the landmark case of *Gideon* v. *Wainwright* (1963).

But even the five-person liberal majority that was finally constituted with Goldberg's appointment in 1962 never completely jelled, because at just about this time Justice Black was becoming increasingly disenchanted with some of the major decisions of that liberal majority. As a result, it was only with the appointment in 1967 of Thurgood Marshall, the first African American to be appointed to the Court, that a strong and solid liberal majority finally came into being. Marshall, the great-grandson of a slave, had served almost his entire legal career as chief counsel to the National Association for the Advancement of Colored People (NAACP) Legal Defense and Educational Fund. In that position, he had mapped the brilliant legal strategy that culminated in the overthrow of legalized segregation in *Brown* v. *Board of Education*. After short periods as a lower federal court judge and as Solicitor General, he was appointed to the Supreme Court by President Johnson, consolidating the liberal majority. Yet only two years later, with the resignation of Chief Justice Warren—who had expected that Lyndon Johnson, not his old California enemy Richard Nixon, would appoint his successor—and the forced resignation of Justice Fortas, due to allegations of quite minor financial improprieties, the Warren Court majority unraveled.

It is important, then, to think about the Warren Court as evolving through several stages. During the first stage, between 1953 and 1962, the liberal minority increased from two (Black and Douglas) to four (adding Warren and Brennan), and most of the Court's decisions continued to be compromises between the different wings of the Court. But the transcendent event during this first stage was the unanimous decision in *Brown* v. *Board of Education* (1954), which had a decisive effect on everything that followed.

Then, after Justice Goldberg was appointed in 1962, the Court at last had a liberal majority, but it was almost immediately weakened by Justice Black's growing disenchantment with the course of Warren Court decisions. Only after Justice Marshall was named to the Court in 1967 was a strong liberal majority finally consolidated, but that majority came apart only two years later with the resignations of Chief Justice Warren and Justice Fortas. President Richard M. Nixon's appointments of Chief Justice Warren E. Burger and Harry A. Blackmun effectively brought the Warren Court era to a close.

A Court of "Outsiders"?

As we shall see, the Warren Court was the first Supreme Court in American history to champion the legal position of the underdog and the outsider in American society. Studying the biographies of the liberal justices, one is immediately struck by the extent to which they were themselves outsiders. Without wishing to suggest that we can reduce complex decisions of the Supreme Court over a period of sixteen years to the social, economic, or psychological backgrounds of the justices, it is still useful to understand the socially marginal origins of all of the liberal justices.

Of the seven liberal justices who served on the Court during 1953–69, six grew up in extremely poor families. Only Brennan had an arguably middle-class background, at least after his father had risen from coal shoveler to prominent labor leader and municipal official.

But Brennan, a Roman Catholic, and his two Jewish colleagues, Goldberg and Fortas, were cultural outsiders who came from immigrant families. Brennan and Goldberg both grew up in families of eight children. Fortas's biographer pointedly emphasizes his outsider mentality and personality. All were excluded from the most lucrative and prestigious areas of private practice because of their religion. Together with the African American Thurgood Marshall, they were all outsiders to the dominant, mainstream, middle-class white Protestant culture.

The three white Protestants, Warren, Douglas, and Black, were all poor as children. Douglas lost his father as a young child. Douglas's family's low social position in Yakima made him, by his own account, sympathetic to the outcasts and underdogs of society; his childhood battle with polio made him, again by his own account, a "loner." Black's father was an alcoholic and eccentric; Black's Southern evangelical background also marked him as a cultural outsider vis-à-vis more "respectable" Protestant sects. Unlike Douglas, who became a professor at Yale Law School, Warren and Black had never been exposed to the culture of the Eastern legal establishment, and always felt a sense of inferiority about their educational backgrounds.

We can briefly contrast the liberal justices with their more conservative brethren. Five conservatives served during at least seven terms of the Warren Court: Tom C. Clark, Felix Frankfurter, John Marshall Harlan, Potter Stewart, and Byron R. White. All were Protestant, except Frankfurter, who was Jewish. Clark, Harlan, and Stewart came from socially prominent upper-middle-class families. Harlan's grandfather had served on the Supreme Court with great distinction. White, like Frankfurter, came from a family of modest means, but both were recognized early for their academic abilities—White studied at Yale Law School; Frankfurter, at Harvard Law School, where he became a professor. An outstanding athlete, White was awarded a Rhodes Scholarship to Oxford University and became a prominent professional football player until his career was interrupted by service in World War II.

If we add to this generally socially mainstream group two other midwestern Protestant conservatives, Harold H. Burton and Charles E. Whittaker, each of whom served as justice on the Warren Court for just about five years, we expand the picture of a group of conservative justices who (except for Frankfurter) were not outsiders, and whose backgrounds gave them good reason to be satisfied with the promise of American life.

While we cannot reduce the revolutionary and complex phenomenon of the Warren Court to the biographies of its justices, it is important to recognize that class, religion, and race all played a role in shaping the men who were to become the Warren Court, and thus in shaping legal history.

II

Brown *v.* Board of Education:

Setting the Themes of the Warren Court

If it had decided nothing else, the Warren Court would be remembered for its unanimous decision in *Brown* v. *Board of Education* (1954), perhaps the most important judgment ever handed down by an American Supreme Court. Coming at virtually the beginning of the Warren Era, the Court's declaration that racial segregation in public schools was unconstitutional became the defining act of Warren Court constitutional jurisprudence, eventually affecting almost every area of constitutional law.

The *Brown* decision represented the dramatic culmination of more than a decade of brilliantly orchestrated legal attacks on segregation by future Supreme Court Justice Thurgood Marshall, then chief counsel to the NAACP Legal Defense Fund. *Brown* initiated a social revolution and served as a catalyst for the civil rights movement led by Dr. Martin Luther King, Jr. However, it also generated a political reaction called "massive resistance," in which virtually every Southern public official declared the *Brown* decision unconstitutional and pledged to disobey it. The Southern response to *Brown* produced the most powerful challenge since the Civil War to the very legitimacy of the Supreme Court and the rule of law.

How the Supreme Court came to decide unanimously that racial segregation is unconstitutional continues to be widely debated. It is surely mistaken to assume that the *Brown* decision was inevitable, or even that it was likely. Until the 1930s, the Court consistently avoided even acknowledging the injustice of the system of racial subordination that had been swiftly reimposed by Southern whites after federal troops were removed from the South in 1877. Under the so-called Compromise of 1877, Southern presidential electors threw their votes to the Republican candidate, Rutherford B. Hayes, in exchange for a promise to remove federal troops stationed in the South since the end of the Civil War. Within a decade, as the rest of the country looked the other way, Southern whites were allowed to retake control of their legislatures and pass Jim Crow laws reimposing a system of racial segregation and subordination on the recently freed slaves.

Despite passage of the Civil War Amendments (Amendments 13, 14, and 15) designed to abolish slavery and extend constitutional protections to the freedmen, the Supreme Court almost from the beginning gave these amendments the narrowest and most unfavorable possible interpretation from the standpoint of protecting the former slaves. For example, the provision in the Fourteenth Amendment guaranteeing blacks the "privileges and immunities" of United States citizens was given such a narrow interpretation in the Slaughterhouse Cases (1873) that it virtually eliminated any future role the clause might have played in constitutional protection of the former slaves. Likewise, the Due Process Clause of the Fourteenth Amendment came to play a vital role in protecting corporations from state regulation, but it was almost never used to support constitutional rights for blacks.

Finally, and most critically for the litigation strategy of the school desegregation cases, in the famous 1896 case of *Plessy* v. *Ferguson* the Supreme Court interpreted the Equal Protection Clause of the Fourteenth Amendment to uphold the system of racial segregation that had been put into place in the South within the previous two decades, on the theory that separation of the races did not necessarily imply inequality. "Separate but equal" had received the imprimatur of the Supreme Court, and the pro-segregation forces marching under that banner relied heavily on the *Plessy* decision in the years to come. Only during the Warren Court, with the overturning of *Plessy* by the *Brown* decision, was the Equal Protection Clause revived as a major source of constitutional rights for blacks and other minorities.

By the end of the nineteenth century, then, the Civil War Amendments had been interpreted to give almost no special constitutional protections to the former slaves, who were originally thought to be their principal beneficiaries. And despite the Fifteenth Amendment, which barred racial discrimination in voting, by the turn of the century virtually all Southern blacks had been disenfranchised, not only by Ku Klux Klan violence and intimidation but also by newly created legal barriers such as poll taxes, literacy requirements, and grandfather clauses (such as that passed by Oklahoma in 1908, which gave the vote to illiterate men only if they were lineally descended from a qualified voter of 1866, a test no black could meet).

The decisions of the Supreme Court narrowing the scope of the Civil War Amendments were initially motivated by judicial fear that generous interpretations of the Amendments would radically alter the traditional decentralized balance of power between federal and state governments. But by the time *Plessy* was decided, the Supreme Court justices had themselves come to absorb and endorse the post-1877 political realities, which conceded to Southern whites a free hand in reestablishing and maintaining what would come to be romanticized as the "Southern way of life."

As Southern white society restored the prewar norm of treating blacks with few legal constraints, recourse to extralegal means such as lynching became widespread. Lynchings not only revealed the violence at the heart of racial subordination but were a grotesque parody of a justice system that had failed its black citizens. The numbers are chilling. Between 1882 (when reliable data was first collected) and 1968, at least 4,743 people were lynched in the United States. The great majority of reported lynchings (73 percent) occurred in the South, and the great majority (also 73 percent) were inflicted upon blacks. Beginning in 1882, there was a steady increase in the number of blacks subjected to extrajudicial murder—from 49 reported lynchings in 1882 to an annual high of 161 a decade later. There then began a slow, long-term decline. From a high of 1,111 during the 1890s, the number of reported lynchings of blacks fell each decade, to 791 during 1900–9, to 561 during 1910–19, to 281 during the 1920s, to 119 during the 1930s—a tenth of what it had been forty years earlier. The 1940s saw only 31 reported lynchings of blacks, and, beginning in the 1950s, most years reported no lynchings. Does this trend indicate a long-term change in Southern racial attitudes even before *Brown* or, instead, does it represent the successful institutionalization of racial domination, making brutal extralegal violence gradually less necessary? This is an important question that requires more study.

As World War II ended, something new and intangible had clearly begun to transform the atmosphere of American race relations. Whether the courage and loyalty of African American troops who fought against Hitler in segregated army units touched the American conscience; or whether Hitler's mass murder of European Jews had finally demonstrated where racist laws might lead; or whether black soldiers, having experienced interracial European societies at first hand, returned home unwilling to accept traditional race relations; or whether American politics was beginning to register the effects of a massive migration of five million disenfranchised Southern blacks to Northern cities, where they were often in a position to tip the balance in closely contested presidential elections—whatever the precise explanation, there clearly appeared a new determination among blacks and some whites in postwar America to end institutionalized racism.

During the 1930s, the success of black sports figures affected American racial consciousness, especially when they defeated Germans, portrayed by Hitler as representatives of a superior

Aryan race. The victory in the 1936 Berlin Olympics of Jesse Owens and the 1938 defeat of German boxer Max Schmeling by the black American heavyweight champion, Joe Louis, had a powerful effect on racial attitudes. Outside the realm of sports, the refusal of the Daughters of the American Revolution to permit the celebrated black opera singer Marian Anderson to perform at their Constitution Hall in 1939 was made a cause célèbre by, among others, Eleanor Roosevelt. An especially committed champion of black causes, Mrs. Roosevelt received the first blacks at the White House since Theodore Roosevelt had condescended to entertain Booker T. Washington, a role model of modest black aspirations for an earlier generation.

In the world of postwar sports, nothing could compare in significance to the decision of the Brooklyn Dodgers baseball team in 1947 to field the outstanding black player Jackie Robinson, thus bringing down the color bar that had excluded even outstanding black athletes from the "great American pastime."

In addition to these developments in popular culture, the 1944 publication of Swedish economist Gunnar Myrdal's *An American Dilemma* galvanized the civil rights movement, becoming a principal authority for the antisegregation campaign. Myrdal's exhaustive two-volume work on the sociology of segregation explicitly called for a legal campaign against school discrimination; his assessment of the damage being done to the black population by Jim Crow laws was later cited in NAACP briefs.

In 1948, some of the most important changes in American political history set the stage for subsequent legal attacks on racial segregation. President Truman, by executive order, desegregated both the civil service and the armed forces, and strengthened and made permanent the Fair Employment Practices Committee, first set up by FDR to end discrimination in hiring. This was enough to induce the South for the first time since the end of Reconstruction to split from the Democratic Party in the 1948 election and run its own candidate, Strom Thurmond of South Carolina, who just barely failed to prevent

Truman's election. The split had already been foreshadowed when the South's veto power within the Democratic Party was broken by President Roosevelt at the 1936 Democratic Convention. At the height of his own political power, Roosevelt was able to demand the end of the requirement that a presidential nominee receive two thirds of the votes of the party convention, a rule that had previously guaranteed a veto to Southern delegates. The South's inability in 1948 to stop Truman with a third-party candidate ended a half century of Southern control of the Presidency.

The NAACP's Strategy for Brown

In 1950, when Thurgood Marshall convinced the NAACP to adopt a pro-integration stance as its official policy, committing the organization to a direct assault on the "separate but equal" standard of *Plessy* v. *Ferguson*, some observers believed that he had embarked on a dangerously high-risk gamble. Persuading the Supreme Court to overrule one of its prior decisions—a rare event—was perhaps the most difficult task an advocate before the Court could set himself. Moreover, recent Supreme Court decisions had seemed to signal that the Court was prepared to hold on a case-by-case basis that the "separate but equal" standard could almost never be met in practice. Only weeks before, in companion cases decided on the same day, the Court had held the Universities of Texas and Oklahoma to a very high standard of equality in the separate accommodations they provided for their black graduate students, deciding that neither university had met the standard. In *Sweatt* v. *Painter*, the Court compared the prestige and marketability acquired by graduates of the all-white University of Texas law school with that obtained by graduates of Texas's newly established black law school, and ordered the admission of black students into the white law school. In *McLaurin* v. *Oklahoma Board of Regents*, the Court examined less tangible benefits of education, invalidating Oklahoma's practice of segregating black graduate students within its university, where the one black student was forced to eat at a separate table and study at a separate desk. In both cases, the Court proved itself willing to extend the requirement of equality in "separate but equal" schools beyond the material aspects of education, such as teacher salaries and school buildings; the Court recognized the intangible, psychological inequalities generated by segregation. *Sweatt* and *McLaurin* were thus promising precedents for an attack on the inequality of the South's segregated school system that would avoid the risks of challenging the "separate but equal" standard head on.

Most segregated black public schools in the South were not even remotely equal to their all-white counterparts even in basic tangible criteria such as dollars spent per pupil; teacher qualifications and salaries; number of pupils per teacher; age and maintenance of school buildings; and number of books in the library. Under any conscientious application of the "separate but equal" standard, most segregated schools were decidedly unequal. So why was it necessary to undertake a direct attack on the "separate but equal" standard now that the Supreme Court had finally seemed to indicate that, in practice, it would virtually never find separate to be equal?

Two, and perhaps three, considerations must have weighed on Thurgood Marshall. First, the Court's implied invitation to litigate the actual inequality of segregated schools on a case-by-case basis would be incredibly costly and time-consuming. Establishing a sufficient trial record in each of the thousands of school districts in America might consume an entire generation of NAACP lawyers, as well as the organization's treasury. Second, and probably more important, was the moral and symbolic significance of conceding the theoretical possibility that there could be racially segregated facilities that would actually be equal. For Marshall, constitutional law was as much about morale and legitimacy as it was about winning individual cases. To win under the *Plessy* standard, the very symbol of the Supreme

Court's historic capitulation to Jim Crow laws, might prove to be really no victory at all. Finally, perhaps Marshall had reflected upon the cycles of American history, in which gains by blacks seemed inevitably to have been followed by periods of reaction, retrenchment, and despair. It may have appeared necessary to Marshall to seize the moment before a future Supreme Court majority might revive the Court's historic indifference to the plight of the descendants of former slaves.

Yet one should not underestimate the risk Marshall's legal strategy posed to the cause of racial equality. In 1953, let alone 1950, there was certainly no assurance that the Supreme Court would be willing expressly to overrule a precedent that had stood for more than a half century. Indeed, when Marshall embarked upon his strategy of overturning *Plessy*, his goal appeared little more than a utopian dream. America, in the midst of anti-Communist paranoia, could hardly have been expected to endorse potential social revolution. The actual membership of the Supreme Court would also not have offered much hope for a radical reversal of constitutional precedent. The most conservative Court since the 1937 New Deal triumph, it seemed to have fallen completely under the sway of Justice Felix Frankfurter's restrictive philosophy of judicial review. It also numbered two Southerners (Justices Black and Clark) as well as two Kentuckians (Chief Justice Vinson and Justice Stanley F. Reed). Except for Black, the other three justices eventually turned out to be among the most resistant to overruling *Plessy*.

Some have argued that Marshall's strategy needs to be understood as involving both maximum and minimum goals. There was no incompatibility, this argument goes, in pursuing the overthrow of *Plessy* while simultaneously recognizing the possibility of retreating to a fall-back position if the Court were unwilling to reverse *Plessy*. This view suggests that one did not need to choose in advance between arguing for overruling the separate but equal standard and arguing for enforcing it more strictly. Perhaps this is true for ordinary litigation, though, even then, the two strategies might require creation of very different—and potentially contradictory—trial records. But where, as here, there was a close relationship between building a social movement and pursuing legal victories, I doubt that it would have been easy to move on both tracks simultaneously.

Suppose that, after four years of litigation, the Supreme Court had reaffirmed the *Plessy* standard and sent the cases before it back to lower courts to determine whether the standard had been satisfied in the particular cases. This would have represented a catastrophic setback for the cause of racial equality, after years in which all hopes had been staked on *Plessy*'s reversal. It would have meant additional years of painstakingly slow lower court litigation before the Supreme Court would ever again have had to decide the issue. Furthermore, the politics of building a strong, long-term civil rights movement required at least occasional victories, of whatever dimension, in order to maintain organizational morale. The Supreme Court's refusal to overrule *Plessy* might have demoralized the civil rights cause for another generation.

Brown I

The *Brown* case was first argued in the Supreme Court during the 1952 term, before Earl Warren succeeded Chief Justice Fred Vinson. There were probably five justices leaning toward overruling *Plessy* after the first argument, but the remaining four— Vinson, Reed, Jackson, and Clark—seemed light-years away from agreeing. Justice Frankfurter succeeded in postponing the case until the next term by requesting reargument specifically directed to the question of the historical scope of the Fourteenth Amendment. After *Brown* was reargued in 1953 with Chief Justice Warren presiding, the Court decided unanimously to overrule *Plessy*. It was as clear to the justices then, as it continues to seem in retrospect, that only a unanimous decision could provide sufficient legitimacy for so grave and far-reaching a reversal of constitutional precedent. Indeed, it was quite possible that any one of the justices initially in favor of reversing *Plessy*—Frankfurter seems the most plausible candidate—might have refused to do so with anything less than a unanimous opinion, out of concern for the institutional legitimacy of the Court. In the process of deciding *Brown*, Frankfurter seems constantly to have struggled against the potential accusation that the decision contradicted his well-known views on judicial restraint.

There are many stories about how Chief Justice Warren patiently brought Justices Reed, Jackson, and Clark aboard. Warren's charismatic but gentle style, nurtured during many successful years in politics, surely helped. Just as important, perhaps, was his opening statement about the case at the justices' first conference after the second argument on *Brown*. In a manner that was eventually to become his judicial trademark, Warren immediately framed the question before the Court as a moral issue, in this case a moral challenge to America to fulfill its unkept promises to its black citizens.

Warren himself looked back on the World War II Japanese internment cases as a defining moment in his life. As California's attorney general, he had supported enforcement of the federal government's order to West Coast officials to remove all American citizens of Japanese descent to concentration camps. In spite of the absence of any evidence of disloyalty or of pro–Japanese Government sentiment, racist stereotypes had substituted for evidence. After he became Chief Justice, Warren movingly remembered witnessing the terrified faces of Japanese American children being removed from their homes and expressed regret for his part in the deportations.

A second explanation of Warren's success in forging a unanimous opinion is that, as a former politician, he brought with him to the Court the ability to balance the competing claims of policy and principle. His *Brown* opinion was drafted to avoid any trace of vindictiveness or moral superiority toward the South. Whatever ambiguities ultimately arose in interpreting *Brown* were the result of Warren's wish to create as extensive a legal and moral consensus as possible.

Reaction to the *Brown* decision was swift. As Richard Kluger recounts in his history of *Brown*, while much of the press outside the South greeted it with enthusiasm, many Southerners were shocked and angered. Some prominent Southern politicians vowed to defy the Court. Senator James Eastland of Mississippi proclaimed that the South "will not abide by or obey this legislative decision by a political court." Senator Harry Byrd of Virginia declared that *Brown* was "the most serious blow that has yet been struck against the rights of the states." And Governor Herman Talmadge of Georgia railed that the Court had "blatantly ignored all law and precedent and usurped from the Congess and the people the power to amend the Constitution, and from the Congress the authority to make the laws of the land." The Justices, he said, had treated the Constitution like "a mere scrap of paper." Finally, Governor Thomas Stanley of Virginia initially promised to take advice from Virginia's "leaders of both races" in responding to *Brown*; only weeks later, though, he shifted to a stance of defiance, vowing that he would "use every legal means at [his] command to continue segregated schools in Virginia."

Some Southerners reacted to the decision with more restraint. The Louisville *Courier-Journal* opined, "The Supreme Court's ruling is not itself a revolution. It is rather acceptance of a process that has been going on a long time. People everywhere could well match the court's moderation and caution." The Atlanta *Constitution* cautioned against heeding "demagogues," telling Atlantans, "It is a time . . . to think clearly."

By contrast, outside the South *Brown* was immediately recognized as a landmark case, and some reports were unabashedly celebratory. *Time* called *Brown* the most important Supreme Court decision since the Dred Scott Case, and said that no other case had "directly and intimately affected so many American families." The Cincinnati *Enquirer* praised the decision by say-

ing, "What the Justices have done is simply to act as the conscience of the American nation." Meanwhile, black America
received the decision quietly and waited to see when and how it
would lead to actual school desegregation.

A Changing Constitution?

In his *Brown* opinion, Warren tiptoed around the question of the
historical legitimacy of *Plessy*'s ruling that "separate but equal"
facilities were constitutional. His opinion left unclear whether
the Court meant to overrule *Plessy* or simply to "distinguish" it
on the basis of changing circumstances. Did the Court mean to
say that *Plessy* was wrong when it was decided, or only that, given
changing moral ideas and social circumstances, the *Plessy* ruling
was no longer appropriate?

Based on what we now know about the Court's delibera-
tions in *Brown*, it is clear that Chief Justice Warren understood
that in order to forge a unanimous opinion, he needed to avoid
any suggestion of condemnation of the South or, indeed, of
Southern practices under Jim Crow laws. To say that racial
segregation had always been unconstitutional—that *Plessy* was
wrong even when it was decided in 1896—meant that the legitimacy of the entire Southern way of life was open to historical
challenge.

As a result, the *Brown* opinion goes out of its way to emphasize
that changing historical circumstances justify a departure from
the "separate but equal" standard. "[W]e cannot turn the clock
back to 1868 when the [Fourteenth] Amendment was adopted,
or even to 1896 when *Plessy* was written," the Chief Justice declared. When the Fourteenth Amendment was adopted, only a
rudimentary system of public education had been established in
America. But circumstances had changed, and widely available
public education—especially in Warren's home state of California—had since become one of the glories of American democracy. "We must consider public education in the light of its full

development and its present place in American life throughout the Nation," Warren concluded.

In addition to recognizing the changing historical importance of public education, Warren suggested that the social and psychological meaning of racial segregation might itself have changed. In *Plessy*, the Court had declared that "the underlying fallacy" of the blacks' argument against segregation lay "in the assumption that the enforced separation of the two races stamps the colored race with a badge of inferiority. If this be so, it is not by reason of anything found in the act, but solely because the colored race chooses to put that construction upon it."

In other words, the *Plessy* Court was insisting that racially segregated facilities were as morally neutral as, for example, separate public rest rooms are for men and women. If a man or woman complained that separate rest rooms stamped him or her with a badge of inferiority, we would tend to suppose that it is solely because that particular person has chosen "to put that construction upon it." The difference is that racial segregation was imposed upon blacks after 1877 as part of an elaborate social system of racial subordination. It was cruel and unjust to assert that any badge of inferiority that blacks experienced because of segregation was only in their minds; that they had simply "cho[sen] to put that construction upon it."

Yet the *Brown* Court did not squarely dispute the correctness of *Plessy*'s analysis of the stigmatization that segregation produced. Instead, Warren declared: "Whatever may have been the extent of psychological knowledge at the time of *Plessy*," the finding that racial segregation implies inferiority "is amply supported by modern authority." The "modern" authorities cited by the Chief Justice in *Brown*'s controversial footnote 11 included sociological and psychological studies designed to prove the intangible harm to a black child's self-esteem that resulted from any system of educational segregation. In turning to the findings of social science, Warren seemed to be suggesting that, because the *Plessy* Court could not have had the benefit of these "modern"

studies, it might actually have been excused for failing to recognize in 1896 that the "badge of inferiority" that segregation
represented was the product of an elaborate system of racial subordination.

Thus, two very different pictures of constitutional interpretation were presented by the Chief Justice in *Brown*. When he
declared that "separate educational facilities are inherently unequal," Warren seemed to be proclaiming that racial segregation
was always unconstitutional, regardless of time and place. This
traditional conception of constitutional interpretation assumes
that constitutional meaning is unchanging, and that what the
Equal Protection Clause of the Fourteenth Amendment meant
when it was adopted in 1868 is what it has continued to mean
today. Under this view, when the Court declared racial segregation unconstitutional in 1954, it also meant that *Plessy* was
wrongly decided in 1896.

A second, opposing, conception of constitutional interpretation was also suggested in Warren's opinion. Under this view,
constitutional meaning changes with changing circumstances. In
Chief Justice John Marshall's famous words from *McCulloch* v.
Maryland (1819), the Constitution is intended "to be adapted to
the various crises of human affairs." Thus, it might be possible
that because of changes in the significance of public education
or in the social meanings attributed to forced racial separation,
changing circumstances can yield changing constitutional, as well
as social, interpretations. Under this view of a "living Constitution," it was imaginable that *Plessy*, though overruled, was once
correctly decided.

It is important to see how these conflicting views affect our
interpretation of the significance of the Warren Court. The first
view, that the Constitution expresses unchanging and "self-
evident" truths, was foreshadowed most eloquently by Thomas
Jefferson in the Declaration of Independence. If the Constitution
outlines "certain unalienable Rights" with which individuals are
"endowed by their Creator," then one would expect a picture of

historically fixed and unchanging constitutional rights. If, however, one expects legal principles to evolve over time depending on changing circumstances or changing moral and legal ideas, then we should avoid speaking of rights as if they are inherent in the nature of things, like the law of gravity. We should recognize instead that constitutional principles, like all legal principles, are inevitably created by judges in accordance with their conceptions of moral values and social needs.

Both views, as we shall see, coexisted in Warren Court constitutional jurisprudence.

Brown II

After deciding that racial segregation in public schools was unconstitutional, the Supreme Court ordered further argument on how its judgment should be implemented. One year later, it handed down *Brown* II, in which it declared that school desegregation should be implemented by lower federal courts "with all deliberate speed."

Some maintain that the real compromise in *Brown* was between the ringing declaration of rights in *Brown* I and the conciliatory statement in *Brown* II, signaling that trial courts could take their time in enforcing the rights of black plaintiffs. In retrospect, there is no question that lower court implementation of the *Brown* decision emphasized deliberateness at the expense of speed. Indeed, many Southern federal trial judges charged with implementing the decision had been appointed to the bench because of their political connections to segregationist senators and shared their patrons' wish to scuttle *Brown*. For them, "all deliberate speed" became the legal formula for doing as little as possible.

The Supreme Court's decision in *Brown* II reflected the justices' understanding that they were initiating a social revolution. The Court feared that because deeply entrenched Southern attitudes and institutions were completely unprepared for immediate desegregation, anything more than a gradualist approach would inevitably lead to violence. As it turned out, however, the opposite approach may have had the better chance of succeeding without violence. Gradualism probably encouraged violence by allowing enough time for opposition to desegregation to build while holding out hope that the decision could be reversed. It took two years before resistance would coalesce into the Southern Manifesto, a document signed by virtually all the senators and congressmen from the eleven states of the old Confederacy. Proclaiming that *Brown* was "contrary to the Constitution," it became the inspiration for the movement for "massive resistance" among Southern elected officials. It also provided encouragement and legitimacy to massive violence and demagoguery, which poisoned Southern politics for another two decades.

Brown II also encouraged Southern public officials to claim that they were performing their legal duties whenever they refused to integrate facilities because there was a threat of violence. Within two or three years after *Brown* I, a deadly cycle of violence and disobedience to court orders had become widespread throughout the South. Judges who issued desegregation decrees feared for their lives. "Impeach Earl Warren" signs appeared throughout the South. And Southern congressmen came within a hair of inducing Congress to pass legislation that for the first time in a century would have severely limited the jurisdiction of the United States Supreme Court.

Cooper v. Aaron (1958)

The massive resistance to the *Brown* decision came to a head in Little Rock, Arkansas, whose demagogic governor, Orval Faubus, deployed the Arkansas National Guard to prevent nine black students from attending Central High School in Little Rock, in flagrant defiance of *Brown* and the desegregation plan ordered by the lower courts. The Little Rock school case, *Cooper* v. *Aaron*, is remembered for its ringing declaration of the Supreme Court's supreme authority to explicate the Constitution. *Cooper* was the first and only Supreme Court opinion ever to be signed individually by all nine justices, underlining their solid determination not to sacrifice constitutional rights to the threat of violence. Faced with clear defiance of the decree of a federal court, President Eisenhower—who had never publicly supported *Brown* and had privately condemned it—was nevertheless compelled to implement the court order by sending federal troops to Central High School. Though there were many other violent forms of resistance to court-ordered desegregation after Little Rock, the South gradually accepted the authority of the federal courts.

III

The Civil Rights Movement

With the decisions in *Brown* I and II, and finally the united front established by the signatures of all nine justices to *Cooper*, it seemed that the Warren Court had taken a position linking it to the emerging civil rights movement. But though it may have been spurred by *Brown* and strengthened by *Cooper*, as the new black movement for social justice evolved it became clear that the Court's response to it was as complex and troubled as that of America in general. As the civil rights movement continued to grow and ever more "sit-in" cases arrived at the Court, Justice Black in particular seemed fearful; increasingly, he voted to punish protesters, threatening the Court's hard-won liberal majority. The history of the civil rights movement during the 1950s and 1960s is thus paralleled by the history of the shifting allegiances of the Warren Court.

The civil rights movement began in 1955 when Rosa Parks refused to take her place in the Negro section of a segregated bus in Montgomery, Alabama. Led by Dr. Martin Luther King, Jr., the movement developed into a national force. In 1963, Dr. King delivered his "I Have a Dream" speech before hundreds of thousands at the Lincoln Memorial in Washington, D.C. A year later, the long-standing power of Southern senators to kill any legislation by filibuster was broken, and the Civil Rights Act of 1964, providing for nondiscriminatory housing and employment, was signed into law by President Lyndon B. Johnson, the first

Southern President since the Civil War. In 1965, Congress passed the Voting Rights Act, which rapidly ended Southern disenfranchisement of blacks and, within an amazingly short time, transformed the entire racial politics of the South.

The tactics of the civil rights movement, ranging from economic boycotts and mass marches to sit-ins at segregated lunch counters in the South, produced a large number of cases before the Supreme Court. The mass marches triggered fears of the breakdown of law and order; and the sit-ins created challenges to the rights of property owners to do as they pleased with their property. Following Mahatma Gandhi's example, Dr. King led the civil rights activists to use civil disobedience as a mechanism for forcing the oppressor to reflect on the nature of that oppression. He thus highlighted a tension in the civil rights movement between insistence on obedience to the Constitution as interpreted by the Supreme Court and acknowledgment of a moral duty to disobey immoral laws. At the very moment that the Court in *Cooper* v. *Aaron* was reminding the citizens of Little Rock of their duty to obey even laws that they disagreed with, Martin Luther King was developing his theory of the legitimacy of disobedience to unjust laws as the centerpiece of the civil rights movement.

Dr. King's appeal to "higher law" demonstrates his willingness to follow the great abolitionist spokesman William Lloyd Garrison in maintaining that an unjust constitutional provision or legal interpretation supporting slavery must yield to God's law. The sense of moral righteousness that empowered the civil rights movement derived its legitimacy not only from the ruling in *Brown* but also from a religiously based higher-law tradition.

But it should not be forgotten that the claim of the civil rights movement to constitutional legitimacy also clearly ignited its moral energy. In America, as Sanford Levinson has reminded us, the Constitution has served as a "civil religion," in which what is constitutional has been regularly confounded with what is morally fundamental. There is no other country in the world, as

Tocqueville perceived, in which the political and the constitutional are so completely interwoven as in America.

The ruling in *Brown* represented almost the first moment since
the Civil War in which the Supreme Court had interpreted the
Constitution wholeheartedly in favor of black aspirations. Armed
with their constitutional text, NAACP lawyers had staked their
entire careers on the proposition that a legally correct interpretation of the Constitution would also prove to be a morally just
interpretation as well.

Desegregation and the First Amendment

The *Brown* decision produced its own dynamic and affected aspects of American constitutional law that did not, strictly speaking, have anything to do with race. The massive resistance pol-
icies of Southern states led them to pass laws that sought to
suppress civil rights organizations, especially the NAACP. These
laws, in turn, were challenged on First Amendment grounds,
producing a new and expansive body of constitutional jurisprudence on the rights of freedom of expression and association,
which gradually transformed the Court's interpretation of the
First Amendment.

In the first stage, Southern officials attempted to destroy the
NAACP by asking to see its membership lists. Under this strategy, those who held government jobs would be immediately dismissed; those in the private sector would be subject to economic
boycotts or threats of violence and intimidation. However, this
strategy was never countenanced by the Supreme Court. In
NAACP v. *Alabama* (1958), the Supreme Court modified a long-
standing practice of deferring to state regulation of organizations
by dramatically expanding the constitutional right of association.
This meant that the NAACP could not constitutionally be compelled to submit its membership lists to government officials.
Again, in *Shelton* v. *Tucker* (1960), the Court struck down an
Arkansas law requiring public school teachers to disclose the

names of organizations in which they held membership. And in *NAACP* v. *Button* (1963), the Court struck down an attempt by the commonwealth of Virginia to prosecute the NAACP for improperly soliciting blacks to serve as plaintiffs in civil rights suits, holding that the NAACP's activities were protected by the First and Fourteenth Amendments.

The attack on civil rights organizations reached its peak at about the same time that the Red Scare (see Chapter 4) produced an all-out governmental assault on the Communist Party and so-called Communist-front organizations. Civil rights cases like *NAACP* v. *Alabama* thus provided among the earliest opportunities for forging a general body of constitutional law strongly protective of the right of political organizations to resist governmental intimidation. These decisions protecting civil rights organizations in turn encouraged the Supreme Court to begin its long and halting process of overturning precedents that had given the federal government, during the previous decade, a virtual blank check to destroy radical organizations. By 1957, the Supreme Court began to express a growing recognition of the contradiction between the developing protections accorded to civil rights organizations and recent Cold War precedents that had rubber-stamped governmental efforts to destroy "subversive" organizations.

The most dramatic illustration of the intersection of the First Amendment and the civil rights movement was the decision in *New York Times Co.* v. *Sullivan* (1964) subjecting state libel laws for the first time to First Amendment scrutiny. The case arose out of a campaign of harassment by Alabama officials to prevent civil rights organizations from raising funds in the North for, among other things, the legal defense of Dr. Martin Luther King, Jr., who had been indicted for perjury in Montgomery, Alabama. The officials brought a libel suit in the Alabama courts against *The New York Times* for several misstatements of fact that appeared in a fund-raising advertisement that the newspaper had published. The threat was clear. If local judges and juries could impose millions of dollars of damages on the preeminent national newspaper for failure to check the factual accuracy of every statement in every advertisement it ran, then no newspaper could ever afford to risk publishing controversial material.

In one of the great opinions of American constitutional law, Justice William Brennan brilliantly reviewed the history of the First Amendment. He focused on the infamous Sedition Act of 1798, which had been enacted by President John Adams's Administration to punish criticism of the Administration. "Although the Sedition Act was never tested in this Court," Brennan declared, "the attack upon its validity has carried the day in the court of history." He thus concluded that the First Amendment bars libel laws from being used to discourage criticism of public officials. "[W]e consider this case against the background of a profound national commitment to the principle that debate on public issues should be uninhibited, robust, and wide-open, and that it may well include vehement, caustic, and sometimes unpleasantly sharp attacks on government and public officials," Brennan wrote in one of his most quoted statements.

In *New York Times Co.* v. *Sullivan*, the state court had awarded damages totaling $500,000 against *The New York Times*, but there were also eleven other pending libel suits by state and local officials seeking an additional $5,600,000 against the *Times*. Five other lawsuits had also been brought against the CBS television network seeking $1,700,000 for its news broadcasts about the advertisement. Fear of damage awards, Brennan observed, might even be greater than fear of criminal punishment under the discredited Sedition Act. "Whether or not a newspaper can survive a succession of such judgments, the pall of fear and timidity imposed upon those who would give voice to public criticism is an atmosphere in which the First Amendment freedoms cannot survive."

Brennan concluded that unless a false statement criticizing a public official could be proved to have been published with "actual malice" or with "reckless disregard" for the truth, First

Amendment freedom of speech principles protected the speaker or writer against damages.

New York Times Co. v. *Sullivan* is a dramatic example of a consciousness-raising phenomenon that occurred quite often during the Warren Era. The struggle over civil rights in the South repeatedly raised questions involving the boundaries of political struggle, as well as the parameters of legitimate criticism of government actions. It was one of the rare periods in American history in which the Supreme Court largely sympathized with the substance of anti-government criticism. In these circumstances, it was much easier to appreciate the deepest meaning of the constitutional guarantees of freedom of speech and association, which through most of its history the Court had managed to ignore.

Justice Black Breaks with the New Liberal Majority

As we have seen, Justice Goldberg's appointment to replace Justice Frankfurter in 1962 signaled a major realignment on the Court. As a result of the replacement of Frankfurter by Goldberg, the new liberal majority dramatically struck down a number of McCarthyite laws as violative of civil liberties. Yet the realignment was less than complete. Shortly after Goldberg was appointed, Justice Black began to distance himself from the newly constituted liberal majority. The issue that first produced a bitter break between Black and his liberal allies was their different reactions to various forms of civil disobedience engaged in by Dr. King and his followers in the civil rights movement.

King had been deeply influenced by the forms of struggle against injustice that the great Indian anticolonial leader Mahatma Gandhi had adopted in his successful campaign to free India from British colonial rule. King also inspired his followers with the declarations of American anti-slavery leaders, who denounced the fugitive slave laws passed under the "slave Constitution" and insisted that there was no duty to obey unjust laws that violated God's law. King was well aware that the "higher law" argument in American history carried the imprimatur of no less sacred a document than Thomas Jefferson's Declaration of Independence, with its "self-evident" truths.

The result was that civil rights activists challenged segregation through a variety of strategies, including mass marches and picketing of courthouses, jails, and other public facilities, as well as sit-ins at lunch counters, restaurants, and motels that refused service to black customers.

Segregation of motels and restaurants created special indignities for black travelers who could never be sure of finding a place to eat, sleep, or relieve themselves. Nevertheless, it was unclear, until Congress passed the Civil Rights Act of 1964, whether these forms of "private" segregation were unlawful, since the Equal Protection clause barred only "state action" that institutionalized segregation. It was in this context that the civil rights movement deployed civil disobedience—not only in order to challenge the injustice of segregation wherever it was found, but also to invoke the Gandhian idea that civil disobedience forces the oppressors to reflect upon the injustice of their actions.

From 1964 through 1966, the Supreme Court heard a number of appeals of criminal convictions of civil rights activists who, after the success of the Montgomery, Alabama, bus boycott of 1955–56, had engaged in sit-ins for the purpose of confronting property owners who maintained segregated facilities. The cases highlighted the historical tensions between law and justice and between property and personal rights with which a radicalized and energized civil rights movement challenged the national conscience.

Was the Court willing to enforce the property rights of owners of segregated facilities even when it meant legitimating laws that most, if not all, of the justices thought were unjust? Was it legitimate for protesters to take the law into their own hands whenever they believed that their own cause was just? In any event, did not the theories of civil disobedience advocated by Dr.

King also imply that in order to confront the oppressors with their own unjust acts the protesters themselves needed to be prepared to suffer the consequences of disobeying unjust laws? Finally, after a decade of disobedience by Southern whites to judicial desegregation decrees, in which the authorities had constantly invoked the obligation to obey the law regardless of one's personal beliefs, how was it now possible to distinguish between the two kinds of civil disobedience? All of these profoundly difficult questions lay behind the Supreme Court considerations of the sit-in cases in which Justice Black first parted company with his liberal allies.

In *Bell* v. *Maryland* (1964), a bitterly divided Court reversed the criminal trespass convictions of civil rights demonstrators who had ignored a request to leave a private Baltimore lunch counter that refused service to blacks. The case was heard by the Supreme Court just as Congress had begun debating the Civil Rights Bill, which was designed to outlaw precisely the kind of segregation in public accommodations that had been challenged throughout the South ever since the first sit-in demonstration at an all-white lunch counter in Greensboro, North Carolina, in 1960. While it was by no means clear that it would be possible to muster enough votes in the Senate to break a Southern filibuster of the bill, it was true that if the bill became law, as eventually it did, sit-ins against segregation would become legitimate. Would it not be ironic for the Court to uphold criminal convictions for activity that was no longer even unlawful? Even more ironically, *Bell* v. *Maryland* was heard by the Supreme Court after the state of Maryland, in response to civil rights protests, had already passed its own public accommodations law that would have made these very sit-ins (if they had occurred later) lawful.

There were basically three positions in the Supreme Court concerning the sit-ins. For Justices Douglas and Goldberg and Chief Justice Warren, segregation in public accommodations was unlawful even without a civil rights act. Turning to the history of the common law involving rights of access to public accommodations and transportation, Douglas maintained that the common law guaranteed nondiscriminatory access to public accommodations even if privately owned. Goldberg and Warren maintained that the Equal Protection Clause itself barred segregation in privately owned facilities. Though each represented a plausible reading of legal history, the Douglas-Goldberg-Warren position ignored the widely held belief that this issue had never been settled and could only be determined by Congress; nor did the justices explain how almost nobody had proposed this argument over the course of an entire century of racially segregated facilities. The rest of the Court, however, assumed that without legislation, there was no legal restriction to prevent owners of private property from engaging in racial discrimination. But that did not settle the issue.

In one sit-in case after another, Justice Brennan managed to muster majority support for opinions reversing the criminal convictions of the civil rights protesters on extremely narrow or technical grounds that avoided reaching the constitutional question concerning the legality of private discrimination. In *Bell* v. *Maryland*, rather than consider the constitutional challenge to legalized segregation in public accommodations, Brennan used the subsequent passage of the Maryland public accommodations law as the basis for vacating the convictions and remanding to the state court to consider the effect of the supervening law. These highly ad hoc grounds seemed designed, above all, to avoid sending the civil rights activists to jail without setting any significant precedent. Brennan, sensitive to symbolic questions of legitimacy, sought to avoid aligning the Supreme Court with racial injustice, even while recognizing that perhaps discrimination in public accommodations was not yet unlawful. Ten days after the Court handed down its decision in *Bell*, the Civil Rights Bill actually did become law. At this point, Brennan's unwillingness to send protesters to jail seems even more justifiable, since they had merely been challenging discrimination that the country itself had finally come to acknowledge was unlawful.

But Justice Black would have none of this. In most of the sit-in cases, he insisted on sending the protesters to jail, expressing contempt for Brennan's efforts to find some hyper-technical basis for reversing the convictions. While one may perhaps agree with Black's long-expressed view that it is not the job of the Supreme Court to substitute "subjective" ideals of justice for the actual law, the civil rights movement also seems to have triggered Black's fears of anarchy and social disorder. In each of his successive opinions in the civil rights cases, his tone became harsher and more angry.

Bell v. *Maryland* left personal scars within the liberal majority that never really healed. After the argument of the case, Black voted with the four conservatives and then wrote and circulated a draft majority opinion to uphold the protesters' convictions. In his draft dissent, Justice Goldberg offended Black by comparing his opinion to the Dred Scott Case, the notorious decision upholding slavery that pushed the nation to the brink of the Civil War. Distrust grew. Black felt that Brennan was delaying release of Black's final opinion out of fear that, as Elizabeth Black put it in her private diary, "Hugo's enormous prestige would work adversely on the [Civil Rights] bill's passage." Soon Black's "scant and scared majority" (in Mrs. Black's words) unraveled, and Justice Brennan managed to produce a 6–3 decision reversing the convictions.

Six months later, in *Cox* v. *Louisiana* (1965), Black once again broke with his former liberal allies in a civil rights case. In December 1961, twenty-three black students were arrested in Baton Rouge, Louisiana, for picketing stores that maintained segregated lunch counters. The following morning, the Reverend B. Elton Cox led a march to the courthouse, where two thousand student demonstrators gathered across the street from the courthouse and jail to protest the arrests. The protesters sang, prayed, and listened to a speech by Cox without incident. However, when Cox urged the crowd to sit in at uptown lunch counters, the sheriff ordered the crowd to disperse, and the police almost immediately fired tear gas shells into the crowd. Cox himself was then arrested. Writing for a 5–4 majority, Justice Goldberg overturned Cox's one-year sentence for "picketing near a courthouse" on the ground "that our constitutional command of free speech and assembly is basic and fundamental and encompasses peaceful social protest."

Goldberg originally had voted in conference to uphold Cox's conviction on the ground that Louisiana was entitled to protect its courts from coercion. But after viewing television film of the march, Goldberg changed his mind, apparently because the local sheriff had seemed at first to permit the protesters to gather in the area near the courthouse. Even so, Goldberg wrote, "The rights of free speech and assembly" do not protect marches "in the middle of Times Square at the rush hour." But granting the police "uncontrolled discretion" to decide when a peaceful march can take place, he concluded, violates the First Amendment.

Once more, at the last moment, Black had lost his majority. His dissent raised the fear that *Cox* would open the door to "fanatical, threatening, lawless mob[s]" applying "coercive pressures" on the courts. "[M]inority groups in particular," he declared, "need always to bear in mind that the Constitution . . . does not take away the State's power, indeed its duty, to keep order and to do justice according to law." In private, Black went even further, denouncing "government by demonstrations and marching." "He remembers Hitler took to the streets before he took over," Mrs. Black recorded in her diary.

Four months after *Cox*, Black reported to his wife that Justice Brennan, among the friendliest and most cordial of justices, "was really mad with him because of one of his opinions and dissents and was very snippy to him in Conference." By the summer of 1965, as terrible riots broke out in the black ghetto of Watts in Los Angeles, Mrs. Black wrote: "Hugo has been saying that the demonstrations would lead to riots and anarchy and he is borne out, to some extent, already." "Part of the lawless spirit of the times," she added two days later, observing that the Los Angeles riots were still going on after three days, with "about 37 killed and 750 wounded and stores burned and looted. Horrible!" The Watts riots exacerbated the fear of Justice Black and others that the civil rights demonstrations were leading only to disorder and unrest. That same summer, Justice Douglas warned newly appointed Justice Fortas that "the majority of the Court [is] moving toward the anti-Negro side," presumably referring to Black's increasing distrust of the civil rights movement. His words were to prove prophetic.

"You can now see what I meant last summer," Douglas told Fortas early in 1966, when Black announced his dissent in another sit-in case, *Brown* v. *Louisiana*. In *Brown*, Fortas led the Court in overturning the breach-of-peace convictions of protesters who sat in at a public library to protest segregated library services. In his impassioned dissent, Black maintained that "[i]t is high time to challenge the assumption in which too many people have too long acquiesced that groups that think they have been mistreated or that have actually been mistreated have a constitutional right to use the public's streets, buildings, and property to protest whatever, wherever, whenever they want, without regard to whom such conduct may disturb . . . But I say once more that the crowd moved by noble ideals today can become the mob ruled by hate and passion and greed and violence tomorrow . . . The peaceful songs of love can become as stirring and provocative as the Marseillaise did in the days when a noble revolution gave way to rule by successive mobs until chaos set in."

Since Black had been brought up in Alabama during its darkest decades of racial oppression, his views on race had for a long time been a subject of intense public scrutiny. No sooner had he been confirmed by the Senate in 1937 than it became public that he had once been a member of the Ku Klux Klan in Alabama. A member of the Klan for two years, and elected to the Senate with its support, Black explained in a public radio address after his confirmation that he had briefly been a Klan member but had long ago resigned. (His biographer records that Black joined the Klan in September 1923 and wrote a letter of resignation in July 1925, though he continued actively to seek the support of Klan members during his 1926 Senate campaign.) His biographers have noted that during his brief tenure as a Birmingham police court judge from 1911 to 1912, he was known for his even-handedness toward blacks. Others, however, have pointed out that as defense counsel in a notorious murder trial of 1921 he had appealed to racial and religious bigotry to win his client's acquittal. In later years, he explained that he joined the Klan largely because many Alabama jurors were also members.

Though he was the only justice from the Deep South, Black was among the small majority of justices who were completely committed to overruling *Plessy* v. *Ferguson* even before Earl Warren became Chief Justice. Black never doubted that there would be turmoil and bitterness when segregation was outlawed. Though he warned Warren that his *Brown* opinion needed to avoid blaming the South, he appears never to have wavered in his view that racial segregation could not be justified under the Fourteenth Amendment. There are many stories involving the personal price Black paid among longtime Southern friends, especially old political friends, who shunned him after *Brown*.

While Black's courageous stand in *Brown* v. *Board of Education* was never in doubt, the civil rights movement engendered deep suspicion from him a decade later. In the sit-in cases he suddenly became a spokesman for the rights of private property—a role that markedly diverged from the populist rhetoric that originally brought him to the United States Senate. It also seemed incongruous with his former position that personal rights were more central to constitutional democracy and thus entitled to greater protection than property rights, which he had argued while battling Justice Frankfurter over the appropriate scope of judicial review.

The Civil Rights Act of 1964 and the Voting Rights Act of 1965 marked the high point of success of the civil rights movement. Thereafter, the public's tolerance of social protest began to wane, especially after Congress seemed to have agreed to the demands of the movement. As Black's dissents illustrated, a continued strategy of civil disobedience triggered fears of lawlessness, just as the challenge to property rights invoked dread of radicalism. Mass marches, especially by blacks, touched deep fears of mob rule. During the summer of 1964, Congress approved the Gulf of Tonkin Resolution supporting President Johnson's escalation of the Vietnam War. The war soon drew energy away from domestic concerns and reversed a decade-long cycle of social reform. During the summer of 1965, the riots in the Watts section of Los Angeles turned many whites against the civil rights struggle.

The changing national mood affected the Supreme Court. In 1966 the Court decided a civil rights case against blacks for the first time since *Brown* v. *Board of Education*. In a second case in 1967, the Court upheld criminal convictions against the leadership of the civil rights movement, including Dr. Martin Luther King, Jr.

In *Adderley* v. *Florida* (1966), Justice Black was finally able to muster a majority in a sit-in case. He aligned himself with the four conservative justices to affirm the convictions of thirty-two students from Florida A & M University in Tallahassee, who had protested outside the county jail against segregation and the arrest of their comrades. The depth of the split within the Court became clear, as Black's defection left his four former liberal allies in dissent. Justice Douglas wrote in the dissenting opinion: "Conventional methods of petitioning . . . for the redress of grievances . . . may be, and often have been, shut off to large groups of our citizens . . . Their methods should not be condemned as tactics of obstruction and harassment as long as the assembly and petition are peaceable, as these were . . . [B]y allowing these orderly and civilized protests against injustice to be suppressed, we only increase the forces of frustration which the conditions of second-class citizenship are generating amongst us."

In the notorious case *Walker* v. *City of Birmingham* (1967), Black again broke with his four liberal colleagues to uphold a contempt of court conviction of Dr. King and other prominent civil rights leaders for disobeying a judicial injunction against engaging in a civil rights demonstration.

The events that led to the decision in *Walker* began in April 1963, when King led a nonviolent campaign to end segregation in public accommodations in Birmingham, Alabama. Birmingham was a particularly dangerous place for the boycott, sit-ins, and marches King proposed, since its chief of police, Eugene "Bull" Connor, was a rabid segregationist who was expected to respond violently to any civil rights demonstrations. But King hoped to draw the nation's attention to the persistence of segregation nearly ten years after *Brown*. After sit-ins and marches in early April resulted in numerous arrests, the city of Birmingham obtained an injunction from an Alabama lower court judge forbidding any further demonstrations. Believing that the injunction was both unconstitutional and immoral, King and the other demonstrators went ahead with marches planned for Good Friday and Easter Sunday. King was promptly convicted of contempt of court for violating the injunction and jailed. While in jail, he learned that eight white Alabama clergymen had issued a statement urging the black community to stop demonstrating and work within the system for reform; in response, he wrote his famous "Letter from Birmingham Jail" outlining his theory of civil disobedience. Explaining his reasons for defying the injunction, he wrote: "I submit that an individual who breaks a law that conscience tells him is unjust, and willingly accepts the penalty by staying in jail to arouse the conscience of the community over its injustice, is in reality expressing the very highest respect for law."

The injunction had been issued by the Alabama judge at a time when much of the state judiciary remained hostile to all civil rights activity. The case was argued before the United States Supreme Court four years later on the assumption that if King had immediately appealed the injunction it would have been overturned as an unconstitutional limitation on First Amendment rights. Therefore, the only question before the Court was whether King was entitled to disobey a concededly unconstitutional judicial order without bringing an appeal.

There was a long history of bitterness by progressives against the use of the injunction by the judiciary to suppress social protest. For almost a half century, the federal courts had issued injunctions against labor union activities, until the practice was barred by Congress in 1932. Widely regarded as the most potent and notorious weapon available to a conservative judiciary hostile to union organizing, the labor injunction provided many advantages to employers. It was issued *ex parte*, meaning that an employer could ask a court to issue an injunction without even initially hearing the employees' position. While the union was free to appeal the injunction, the appeal took time and money. The injunction thus had the effect of cooling down the energy, solidarity, and shared sense of injustice that might have taken a long time to build. Employers quickly realized what an effective instrument the injunction was for demobilizing social protest movements. Equally important, disobedience to an injunction could be punished as contempt of court by a judge without a jury, thus eliminating any restraint that juries drawn from a community might have exercised on unpopular criminal convictions.

The use of the injunction against the demonstrators in *Walker* v. *City of Birmingham* brought to mind the partisan uses of the injunction to squelch labor unions. Nor could the Supreme Court justices have failed to remember that for more than a decade they had struggled against Southern judges who applied the law in bad faith in order to thwart school desegregation or to attempt to crush the NAACP. To appeal an injunction through a hostile state judiciary all the way to the United States Supreme Court could take years. The appeal in *Walker* itself took four years. Could the Supreme Court really have expected civil rights protesters to suspend their activities during that period? The Supreme Court ruling in *Walker* thus empowered local Southern judges to tie up the civil rights movement in the expensive and time-consuming task of overturning illegitimate court-ordered injunctions.

"It cannot be presumed," Justice Potter Stewart declared for the majority, "that the Alabama courts would have ignored the petitioners' constitutional claims." In other words, the Court was no longer willing to suppose—as it had frequently done during the previous decade—that Southern judges were doing their best to crush the civil rights movement.

As Chief Justice Warren declared in dissent, the Court was giving its "seal to . . . a gross misuse of the judicial process." "This injunction was such potent magic that it transformed the command of an unconstitutional statute into an impregnable barrier" that could be challenged only through "protracted legal proceedings." The civil rights marchers, he wrote, "were in essentially the same position as persons who challenge the constitutionality of a statute by violating it and then defend the ensuing criminal prosecution on constitutional grounds. It has never been thought that violation of a statute indicated such a disrespect for the legislature that the violator always must be punished even if the statute was unconstitutional . . . Indeed, it shows no disrespect for law to violate a statute on the ground that it is unconstitutional and then to submit one's case to the courts with the willingness to accept the penalty if the statute is held to be valid."

In his own dissenting opinion, Justice Brennan wrote, "We cannot permit fears of 'riots' and 'civil disobedience' . . . to divert our attention from what is here at stake." *Walker* suggests that by 1967 a majority of the Supreme Court had been infected by those fears. The Court was no longer willing to presume that the civil rights movement's acts of civil disobedience were legitimate and should be treated with impunity. The country at large had become more intolerant of social protest, as it faced the prospect of a long-drawn-out land war in Asia. As widespread rioting in black ghettos during the "long hot summer" of 1967 led to the recognition, in the words of the Kerner Commission on Civil Disorder, that racial polarization was dividing the country into "two nations," the hope that had led to a decade of social reform was replaced by growing despair that the United States would ever be able to overcome the heritage of slavery. On April 4, 1968, less than five years after delivering his "I Have a Dream" speech, Martin Luther King lay dead, the victim of an assassin's bullet.

How had the civil rights movement changed American law and society? Two cases decided toward the end of the Warren Court era show the conflicted legacy of *Brown*. Just the day before King's assassination, the Court heard argument in a lawsuit challenging the "freedom of choice" plan adopted by New Kent County, Virginia, for its public schools. The facts in *Green* v. *County School Board of New Kent County* reveal the pervasiveness of racial segregation fourteen years after *Brown*.

Until 1965, New Kent County had continued to maintain a segregated dual school system for the more than 50 percent of its population who were black. Faced with a cutoff in federal financial aid, the county then adopted a "freedom of choice" plan for desegregating its schools, under which students were allowed to choose whether to attend the all-black school or the all-white school. During the plan's three years of operation, even though there was no residential segregation, no white student had chosen to attend the all-black school, while only 15 percent of the black students had chosen—or dared—to move to the formerly all-white school. For whatever complex combination of reasons, racially segregated public schools had continued to be the rule not only in New Kent County, Virginia, but in most of the United States, North and South. More than forty years after *Brown*, *de facto* segregation in housing and schools is still prevalent throughout the country.

On the other hand, *Brown*'s challenge to racism ameliorated some of its more vicious manifestations. For example, interracial marriages are no longer beyond the pale for most Americans. In 1967, when sixteen states still had laws barring interracial marriage, the Warren Court struck down a Virginia anti-miscegenation statute as a violation of equal protection. Surprisingly, there was almost no negative public reaction to the decision in *Loving* v. *Virginia*. It had long been feared that school desegregation would bring to the surface all the repressed terrors associated with the specter of interracial sex, a specter that had always played a major part in American race relations. White slaveholders had a history of sexual abuse of women slaves; guilt over that history may have accounted for some of the brutality with which Southern white men treated black men accused of making sexual overtures to white women. Accusations of sexual assaults on white women were a common pretext for lynchings of black men. Black men accused of raping white women also received stiffer prison sentences, and were many times more likely to receive the death penalty, than if the defendant was white or the victim black.

The NAACP's litigation strategy for school desegregation was carefully crafted to minimize fears of miscegenation. The first cases brought to the Supreme Court challenging school segregation were limited to graduate education on the assumption that there would be less resistance to racial mixing among mature graduate students. For several years after *Brown* was decided, Justice Frankfurter devoted considerable energy to throwing procedural roadblocks in the way of deciding whether *Brown* extended to overturning anti-miscegenation laws. He worried that any acknowledgment by the Supreme Court that interracial marriage was legalized after *Brown* would fuel demagogic white charges of "racial mixing."

Given the history of fears of interracial sex, the mild reaction to *Loving* v. *Virginia* is an important measure of the extent to which *Brown* shook up deep cultural assumptions about race. *Loving* was decided just two years after a constitutional right to marital privacy had been recognized in *Griswold* v. *Connecticut*. By then the idea that the state could meddle in the intimate realms of marriage, even in the name of racial line-drawing, had become deeply suspect. Even racists were no longer prepared to defend state interference with one's freedom to choose a marriage partner.

IV

Standing Up to McCarthyism

When Senator Joseph R. McCarthy of Wisconsin delivered his notorious Wheeling, West Virginia, speech on February 9, 1950, claiming—but never proving—that there were a large number of Communists in the United States government, he formally inaugurated what came to be called McCarthyism. It is misleading, however, to think of the anti-Communist hysteria that gripped the United States during the 1950s as the work of any one person. Though McCarthy was an appalling liar and a cynical manipulator of popular anxieties, it is wrong simply to demonize him. The historical explanation of the McCarthy Era must recognize the broad social forces that were at work, beyond the influence of any single individual. Without the active collaboration of many people—including future President Richard M. Nixon, then an unknown second-term congressman, as well as much of the conservative Republican establishment led by Ohio Senator Robert A. Taft—and the passive acquiescence of many others, McCarthy could never have become the prominent and powerful demagogue after whom an entire era was named.

Dated in terms of the life of the junior senator from Wisconsin, the McCarthy Era would have ended not long after it began. Unknown outside Wisconsin before his 1950 speech, McCarthy saw his political fortunes begin to decline just four years later, when he rashly attacked President Eisenhower and the United States Army for being "soft on Communism." The Army-

McCarthy hearings marked the end of McCarthy's period of greatest influence. From that time on, he was increasingly abandoned even by his own Republican Party. After the Senate passed a resolution condemning McCarthy, in 1954, he rapidly degenerated into acute alcoholism, and died in 1957. As measured by McCarthy's own personal influence, then, the McCarthy Era lasted hardly five years.

In fact, however, the anti-Communist hysteria that bears the name McCarthyism began well before McCarthy's entry onto the scene and did not end until long after his death. The hysteria led to a large number of undocumented attacks on the loyalty of individuals and organizations: on Communists, former Communists, and "fellow travelers"; on government and union officials; and on Hollywood actors, screenwriters, and many other artists. Numerous government officials were dismissed from their jobs without a hearing or any proof or documentation of their alleged "disloyalty," including many homosexuals who were dismissed as "security risks." Dishonorable discharges of gays in the armed forces also greatly increased, for the same reason. Many scientists and engineers had their professional lives destroyed by denial of security clearances necessary for working in defense-related industries. High-school teachers and university professors were thrown out of jobs without knowing who had accused them or of what they had been accused. Some had refused as a matter of conscience to sign loyalty oaths, which rapidly proliferated as a condition of employment required by federal, state, and local governments. Many people were denied passports to travel abroad. Others who had lived most of their lives in the United States but had never become American citizens were summarily expelled from the country without any formal legal proceedings. Foreigners were frequently barred from entering the United States to lecture, travel, or study.

The origins of McCarthyism can be traced to the emergence of the Cold War, as the World War II alliance against Nazism between the United States and the Soviet Union began to collapse. From the time of former British Prime Minister Winston Churchill's famous 1946 warning that an iron curtain was descending across Europe, the level of postwar American anxiety had begun to soar. Within a very short time, the Soviets took control of Eastern Europe and aided the Communists in the Greek civil war. The announcement in 1949 that the Soviet Union had tested an atomic bomb, years before anyone in the West had imagined this could happen, dramatically punctured the sense of security that two oceans had for so long provided. It also encouraged demagogues like McCarthy to contend that the Soviets had received the secret of the bomb from spies inside the U.S. government. McCarthy's cry that there had been "twenty years of treason" dating all the way back to the beginning of Roosevelt's New Deal was initially greeted with enthusiasm by his fellow Republicans. The newly powerful discourse of American anti-Communism promulgated by McCarthy was welcomed by the right as a means of attacking the New Deal and its legacy.

The fall of China to the Communists in 1949 and the invasion of South Korea by Communist North Korea in 1950 magnified the feeling that the world was falling to the Communists. The American-led defense of South Korea soon triggered a massive Chinese Communist intervention in the Korean War and, for a time, raised the real possibility of an American military defeat. Anti-Communist hysteria spread throughout the United States, as a "witch-hunt" for domestic traitors and spies served the psychological function of displacing responsibility for foreign military and diplomatic disasters.

Though anti-Communism had been a feature of American political life since the Russian Revolution of 1917, the new hysteria demanded ever more elaborate mechanisms for seeking out and destroying imagined enemies within. Much of the repressive machinery that had been put into place before the Second World War for rooting out Nazi and Fascist spies was rapidly redeployed against Communist and leftist opponents. To give three major examples: the House Un-American Activities Committee

(HUAC), originally created in 1938 to monitor pro-German elements in the United States as well as Communist activity, stepped up the pace of its investigations, turning all its force against suspected Communists and "fellow travelers."

The Smith Act, passed in 1940 as the United States and the Soviet Union were becoming allies, made it a criminal offense to advocate the violent overthrow of the United States government or to join any organization that advocated it. The Smith Act was used to prosecute members of the Socialist Workers Party as early as 1941, but was rarely used during World War II. It was dusted off in 1948 to prosecute eleven of the top leaders of the American Communist Party, who were sentenced to substantial jail terms.

And the director of the Federal Bureau of Investigation, J. Edgar Hoover, quickly realized that he could massively expand his organizational and personal power by shifting from an anti-crime to an anti-Communist mission, while using national security as an excuse to build files based on surveillance and wiretapping of domestic "security risks." Until his death in 1972, these files enabled Hoover to blackmail and terrorize politicians and public officials.

Two highly publicized trials involving accusations of espionage heightened and focused anti-Communist hysteria. After Alger Hiss was convicted of perjury in 1950 for denying that he had transmitted official documents to an admitted ex-Communist, Whittaker Chambers, the American public was prepared to believe that Communist sympathizers and spies were everywhere. A graduate of the Harvard Law School, and law clerk to Justice Oliver Wendell Holmes, Hiss had risen to a high-ranking State Department position. There were virtually no other proven examples of disloyalty at Hiss's level, and Hiss himself always maintained that he was framed. Nevertheless, his conviction (in a second trial, after a hung jury refused to convict in the first) seemed to confirm McCarthyite accusations of pro-Soviet infiltration of the highest levels of the United States government and, especially, of widespread disloyalty among the privileged Eastern establishment.

By 1953, when Julius and Ethel Rosenberg were executed after having been convicted of delivering the secret of the atomic bomb to a Soviet agent—an accusation apparently without scientific merit—Americans were experiencing a deep loss of control in a world that seemed to be turning against them. After Chief Justice Vinson, in an unprecedented move, hastily reconvened the Supreme Court during its summer recess to overturn Justice Douglas's stay of the Rosenbergs' execution, it appeared that even the high court had been swept up by the anti-Communist hysteria.

The Supreme Court, McCarthyism, and the First Amendment

In 1949, just as anti-Communist fervor was approaching its peak, Justices Frank Murphy and Wiley B. Rutledge died within two months of each other. During the previous six years, along with Justices Black and Douglas (and, until he died in 1946, Chief Justice Stone), they had formed the most solid pro–civil liberties block in the history of the Supreme Court. The deaths of Murphy and Rutledge, at a time when President Truman was capitulating to congressional anti-Communist demagoguery, allowed Truman to appease right-wing forces by appointing two conservative justices, Tom C. Clark and Sherman Minton. Clark and Minton substantially strengthened the conservative wing of the Supreme Court led by Justice Felix Frankfurter. During some of the worst infringements on civil liberties in American history, the Frankfurter wing was ready to uphold virtually every repressive governmental measure justified in the name of national security.

Frankfurter believed that judicial restraint was necessary in order for the Court to retain its legitimacy in a constitutional democracy. He had developed these views in reaction to the so-called *Lochner* era of the early twentieth century, when the Supreme Court had intruded into the political process to strike down as unconstitutional laws that were designed to reform the economic and social system. It was Frankfurter's position that the Court could retain its own influence and prestige only by deferring to legislative judgment, except where the legislature had acted completely unreasonably. The result of these views during the McCarthy Era was that the Court simply rubber-stamped congressional and state laws that interfered with freedom of speech and expression.

The most notorious example of the Court's capitulation to the forces of repression occurred in *Dennis v. United States* (1951), in which the eleven top leaders of the American Communist Party were convicted under the Smith Act for advocating the violent overthrow of the United States government. The case raised the question of whether individuals could be convicted for mere speech, and, if so, whether there were constitutional limits on the government's power to punish speech. By a 6–2 vote, the Court upheld the conviction. The leading opinion by Chief Justice Vinson, another of Truman's appointees, seemed to undermine thoroughly the "clear and present danger" test for determining under what circumstances government could interfere with speech.

Since the "clear and present danger" standard will preoccupy us throughout our study of Warren Court decisions involving freedom of expression, we should pause for a moment and try to understand the constitutional issues that the Court faced. Justice Oliver Wendell Holmes originally formulated the "clear and present danger" test in *Schenck v. United States* (1919) for the purpose of distinguishing between constitutionally protected speech and speech that fell outside the protection of the First Amendment and could thus be punished. Holmes's famous example of falsely shouting "Fire" in a crowded theater was designed to illustrate the kind of speech that presented such a clear and present danger of causing injury that it could legitimately be punished. Under the "clear and present danger" test, speech could not be punished unless it raised the threat of *substantial* and *imminent* danger. In a series of dissenting opinions during the 1920s involving governmental punishment of radical political speakers, Holmes and Justice Louis D. Brandeis unsuccessfully sought to persuade a majority of the justices that freedom of expression was a paramount constitutional value that deserved extensive judicial protection. The "clear and present danger" standard, they argued, was the best means of encouraging a "free trade in ideas" while fostering democratic citizenship.

When a New Deal majority was finally established after 1937, it was forced to confront the status of the Holmes-Brandeis free speech dissents. The question of whether the Constitution accorded a "preferred position" to First Amendment protections of freedom of expression almost immediately split the new majority. Justices Rutledge and Murphy, along with Black and Douglas, favored increased protection of First Amendment freedoms. On the other hand, Justice Frankfurter, who had long opposed judicial activism in striking down social and economic legislation, maintained that consistency required equal judicial deference to legislation affecting freedom of speech.

By the time the Supreme Court upheld the criminal convictions of the top American Communist leaders in *Dennis*, two years after the deaths of Rutledge and Murphy, Frankfurter's position held sway. Only Justices Black and Douglas, the two dissenters in *Dennis*, still held the Holmes-Brandeis view that the Constitution accorded a preferred position to the First Amendment. While Chief Justice Vinson's majority opinion in *Dennis* purported to adopt the "clear and present danger" standard proposed by Holmes and Brandeis, it actually eviscerated that standard by ignoring whether the danger was "imminent." In his concurring opinion in *Dennis*, Frankfurter rejected the "clear and present danger" test in favor of a balancing test, weighing the government's interest in suppressing speech against the individual speaker's First Amendment interest. Such a test gave the government much more leeway to enact measures repressive of political speech. *Dennis* marked the low ebb of Supreme Court protection of free speech after World War II.

"Red Monday," 1957: The Court Puts Limits on McCarthyism

Until Justice William Brennan took his seat in 1956, the Frankfurter position dominated the Court's free speech jurisprudence. But there was a dramatic shift during the 1956–57 term, Brennan's first on the Court, as the Supreme Court handed down a series of decisions that began to turn the tide against McCarthyite legislation. Within a few years, as we shall see, Justice Brennan became the major intellectual force on the Court in shaping and extending constitutional protections of freedom of expression well beyond any point that Holmes, Brandeis, or Stone could ever have thought possible.

The most important case decided during the 1956–57 term was *Yates* v. *United States*, in which the Supreme Court overturned Smith Act convictions of the so-called second-string Communist leaders. *Yates* was one of several major cases decided on the last day of the term—denounced as "Red Monday" by its opponents—that signaled that the Court was finally prepared to move against McCarthyism. Justice John Marshall Harlan, a conservative appointed three years earlier by President Eisenhower, wrote a narrow and technical opinion that cast doubt on whether the Court would ever again sustain prosecutions of Communists under the Smith Act. The core of the Harlan opinion was that since the First Amendment protected advocacy "of abstract doctrine," as opposed to advocacy of direct action against the government, the evidence against the *Yates* defendants was too weak to warrant a conviction.

In another major decision delivered on "Red Monday," *Watkins* v. *United States*, Chief Justice Warren for the first time set limits on the investigative power of the House Un-American Activities Committee, which had developed into one of the central institutions for exploiting anti-Communist hysteria. One can trace the rising curve of its influence. A decade earlier, few members of the House of Representatives had wanted to serve on the Committee; by the time *Watkins* was decided, publicity-hungry congressmen were lining up for assignment to HUAC, and similar investigative committees had been established in the Senate.

HUAC's most important function was to hold public hearings at which those who were willing to recant their Communist-sympathizing past were required to engage in public repentance and self-humiliation. Sincere repentance was largely determined by witnesses' willingness to "name names" of those who had participated with them in a suspect organization. For those whose consciences would not permit them to involve others, a very different ritual evolved. These unwilling witnesses typically pleaded the Fifth Amendment, claiming that their refusal to testify was based on the concern that they might incriminate themselves by offering testimony that could subsequently be used against them in a criminal trial. Senator McCarthy regularly denounced these witnesses as "Fifth Amendment Communists," and many of them were fired from their jobs after invoking their constitutional rights.

Those who did plead the Fifth Amendment before either HUAC or the multiplying number of other congressional committees that joined in the chase were faced with another dilemma. The legal rule that one could not answer some questions and "plead the Fifth" to others forced witnesses to invoke the Fifth Amendment from the beginning of their testimony. Congressional investigators made the most of the spectacle of witnesses who repeatedly claimed their Fifth Amendment privilege in answer to a series of seemingly innocent questions. Those witnesses who stood on their consciences by refusing to name names were portrayed as completely uncooperative and contemptuous of Congress. As the television era was dawning, the image of "Fifth Amendment Communists" as unreasonably hostile to congressional inquiries reached the entire nation. In fact, while these witnesses might have been willing to testify about their own past activities, any cooperation might trap them into having to answer every question, which would inevitably involve others.

Some witnesses, who were unwilling to misrepresent their reasons for refusing to answer by "claiming the Fifth," which could only be legitimately invoked out of personal fear of future prosecution, took the courageous step of claiming instead a First Amendment right of freedom of expression. Claiming the protection of the First Amendment was risky; many who did so were convicted of contempt of Congress and jailed. In fact, contempt citations were issued with hitherto unheard-of frequency during the McCarthy Era. During the 150 years from 1792 to 1942, only 108 contempt citations were issued, fewer than one per year; during the brief period 1945–57, HUAC alone issued 135 contempt citations. Playwright Arthur Miller was one of the many convicted of contempt of Congress (his conviction was later overturned) for declining on the ground of irrelevancy to answer some of HUAC's questions about people he had known in the past. HUAC's power to issue contempt charges provided a major incentive for witnesses to comply with its demands.

Chief Justice Warren's opinion in *Watkins* v. *United States* marked the first time that the Supreme Court had interfered with the witch-hunting powers of a congressional committee. As a direct challenge to congressional power, it represented a politically dangerous move by a Court already faced with mounting "massive resistance" in the South to the *Brown* decision. Thus, it should come as no surprise that Warren's opinion, like Harlan's in *Yates*, was based on narrow and technical grounds.

Warren did not deny a broad power in Congress to authorize any investigation into Communist subversion that it wished. The problem in *Watkins*, he said, was that there was no clear authorization by the House of Representatives to HUAC to conduct this particular investigation. "[T]here is no congressional power to expose for the sake of exposure," Warren wrote. Thus, while it was still theoretically possible after *Watkins* for the House simply to authorize every future HUAC investigation, the decision forced every member of Congress for the first time to take personal responsibility for the outrages committed by congressional witch-hunters. Barely a month after Senator McCarthy's death, Chief Justice Warren probably sensed that the tide had already begun to turn and that HUAC was becoming an embarrassment to many congressmen, who might no longer be willing to vote blank checks to the Committee.

1957–62: The Court in Retreat

The Court's 1957 shift turned out to be temporary; it would be misleading to conclude that its "Red Monday" decisions constituted a sudden victory over McCarthyite legislation. Until 1962, when Arthur Goldberg's appointment finally did shift the balance of power on the Court, a solid five-person majority continued regularly to uphold Cold War legislation.

One set of cases strikingly illustrates the Court majority's continuing reluctance to interfere with repressive governmental action. In *Konigsberg* v. *State Bar of California* (1957) (*Konigsberg* I), Justice Black reversed a decision of the California Bar Examiners refusing Raphael Konigsberg a license to practice law after he declined to answer questions directed at finding out whether he had ever been a Communist. In another quite technical opinion based on rules of evidence, Black held that the Bar Examiners made unwarranted inferences of bad moral character from Konigsberg's failure to answer. He sent the case back to the examiners to reconsider their conclusion.

Four years later, in *Konigsberg* II (1961), after the state bar once again rejected Konigsberg's petition for admission, the Court, in a 5–4 opinion by Justice Harlan, upheld the Bar Examiners' decision to refuse Konigsberg a license to practice law. This time the Bar Examiners rested their refusal on the slightly different ground that Konigsberg's refusal to answer had obstructed the Committee's investigation, not that it directly illustrated bad moral character. It appears that the Court was backing away from *Konigsberg* I.

In three other major areas, a five-person Cold War majority continued to endorse politically repressive governmental measures during the years immediately before Arthur Goldberg replaced Justice Frankfurter in 1962. As late as 1961, Justice Harlan wrote an opinion in *Scales* v. *United States* that applied his earlier distinction between "advocacy in the abstract" and "advocacy of action" to uphold a conviction under the Smith Act of the chairman of the North and South Carolina Communist Party. The widespread assumption that Harlan's earlier reversal of the convictions of the "second-string" leaders of the Communist Party in *Yates* had signaled the end of Smith Act convictions turned out to be mistaken. Harlan would be remembered for writing the last opinion upholding a conviction of someone sent to jail under the Smith Act. Indeed, one can be confident that if the *Scales* case had come before the Supreme Court only one year later, the four dissenters in *Scales*—Warren, Black, Douglas, and Brennan—would have been joined by newly appointed Justice Goldberg to overturn Scales's conviction.

Similarly, in a second 5–4 decision in 1961, *Communist Party* v. *Subversive Activities Control Board*, Justice Frankfurter upheld the forced registration of the Communist Party under another McCarthyite law, the Internal Security Act or Subversive Activities Control Act of 1950 (generally known as the McCarran Act). Even though registration brought real potential harm to members of the Party, including denial of tax exemptions, denial of passports, labeling of mail, possible self-incrimination, restrictions on employment in defense plants or labor unions, and disqualification from naturalized citizenship, Justice Frankfurter called these "abstract assertions of possible future injur[ies]," too hypothetical to consider in the present case. Frankfurter's decision would nevertheless prove to be the swan song of the

McCarran Act, just as *Scales* had been for the Smith Act. After Goldberg's appointment in 1962, the Court never again upheld enforcement of McCarran Act provisions against an American citizen.

The Court also reverted to Cold War orthodoxy after 1957 in cases challenging the constitutionality of legislative investigations. In *Barenblatt* v. *United States* (1959), the Cold War majority virtually ignored Chief Justice Warren's *Watkins* opinion. A 5–4 decision by Justice Harlan upheld a contempt citation against a university instructor who stood on his First Amendment rights of freedom of speech and association in refusing to answer HUAC questions about his political beliefs. Harlan not only refused to apply the *Watkins* analysis but contemptuously dismissed Warren's declaration that "there is no congressional power to expose for the sake of exposure." Harlan applied a "balancing test" to conclude that the governmental interest in national security outweighed Barenblatt's First Amendment rights.

Unlike his liberal brethren, who suspiciously reviewed all Cold War legislation on the assumption that it constituted a dangerous threat to civil liberties, Harlan basically accepted the legitimacy of Cold War measures aimed at the Communist Party. It was justifiable to single out the Communist Party for special persecution, Harlan announced. "[T]his Court . . . has consistently refused to view the Communist Party as an ordinary political party, and has upheld federal legislation aimed at the Communist problem which in a different context would certainly have raised constitutional issues of the gravest character."

How do we account for the tortuous process by which the Court between 1959 and 1962 seemed to flee from its earlier anti-McCarthy initiatives? What induced Justices Harlan and Frankfurter, who in 1957 concurred in several of these anti-McCarthy decisions, suddenly to forge a solid and inflexible bloc of five that regularly rubber-stamped all manner of repressive governmental activity?

The explanation seems to be the Jenner-Butler Bill, a "drastic anti-Court measure" that represented the immediate congressional reaction to "Red Monday." During the summer of 1957, a coalition of McCarthyite legislators and Southern opponents of *Brown* sought to retaliate against the Supreme Court by introducing legislation that would have brought about the most significant reduction in the Court's appellate jurisdiction since the post–Civil War years, barring the Court from accepting or deciding cases in areas where its rulings had angered conservative members of Congress. One year later, the proposal was defeated in the Senate by a vote of 49–41. As one commentator noted: "The Court had escaped by the skin of its teeth; the . . . bill was clearly the high-water mark of congressional hostility to the Warren Court."

1962–69: The Demise of McCarthyism
With Frankfurter's retirement and Goldberg's appointment in 1962, the Court once again had a pro–civil liberties majority. After 1962, the Court never again upheld punishment of an individual for refusing to answer questions before a legislative committee investigating Communist activities.

In a series of cases after Goldberg's appointment, the Court indicated it would no longer enforce provisions of the McCarran Act. Directly overruling Frankfurter's position in *Communist Party* v. *Subversive Activities Control Board*, it refused on self-incrimination grounds to force Communist Party members to register under the Act in *Albertson* v. *Subversive Activities Control Board* (1965). It also struck down as a violation of the right to travel a provision of the Act denying passports to Party members in *Aptheker* v. *Secretary of State* (1964). And in *United States* v. *Robel* (1967), it held that the Act's provision barring all members of Communist-front organizations, "without regard to the quality and degree of membership," from being employed in defense plants was unconstitutionally overbroad.

By this time, it had become common for Southern opponents

of desegregation to accuse civil rights organizations of being infiltrated by Communists. Perhaps the most dramatic immediate result of Goldberg's appointment was to prevent this strategy from ever being endorsed by the Court. The outcomes of two specific 1962 term cases dealing with harassment of the NAACP were actually reversed when Goldberg replaced Frankfurter after the cases had already been argued and voted on. In *Gibson* v. *Florida Legislative Investigation Committee* (1963), a Florida legislative investigating committee sought to harass the Miami branch of the NAACP by ordering it to turn over its membership list on the grounds that it had been infiltrated by Communists. Reargument transformed what had been a 5–4 decision upholding the committee's power into a 5–4 opinion written by Justice Goldberg holding that the committee had violated the organization's First Amendment rights.

In *NAACP* v. *Button* (1963), where the commonwealth of Virginia had attempted to ban the NAACP under a statute forbidding improper solicitation of legal business, Frankfurter had already prepared a draft majority opinion upholding the Virginia law. Reargument after his retirement resulted in a victory for the NAACP on First Amendment grounds, a decision Frankfurter bitterly criticized, saying it resulted from the appointment of "such wholly inexperienced men as Goldberg . . . without familiarity with . . . the jurisprudence of the Court either as practitioners or scholars or judges."

Nevertheless, it was only in 1969, the last year of the Warren Court, that the Holmes-Brandeis free speech position completely triumphed. In *Brandenburg* v. *Ohio*, the Court unanimously overturned the conviction of a leader of the Ohio Ku Klux Klan, who had been prosecuted under that state's criminal syndicalism statute, which barred joining any organization "to teach or advocate the doctrines of criminal syndicalism." Criminal syndicalism laws were widely adopted between 1917 and 1920 as part of the "Red Scare" that swept America after the Russian Revolution, and specifically targeted the Industrial Workers of the World, a radical labor group. In *Whitney* v. *California* (1927), the Supreme Court had upheld California's criminal syndicalism law—very similar to Ohio's—saying, " 'advocating' violent means to effect political and economic change involves such danger to the security of the State that the State may outlaw it." (Holmes and Brandeis had dissented on the basis of the "clear and present danger" test, which might have exonerated the defendant.) In *Brandenburg*, the Court decisively rejected the line of cases culminating in *Whitney* as "thoroughly discredited," and adopted the reasoning of the Holmes-Brandeis dissents. *Brandenburg* marked the triumph of the Holmes-Brandeis position that First Amendment freedoms could be abridged only in the case of a clear and present danger. "The constitutional guarantees of free speech and free press," the Court wrote, "do not permit a State to forbid . . . advocacy of the use of force . . . except where such advocacy is directed to inciting or producing imminent lawless action and is likely to incite or produce such action."

Justice Brennan's Contribution to First Amendment Jurisprudence

Justice Brennan joined the Court in 1956 at one of the darkest moments in the history of civil liberties. As we have seen, for the previous seven years a solid majority, led by Justice Frankfurter, had rubber-stamped all manner of Cold War governmental measures designed to combat subversive activities. The only resistance on the Court came from Justices Black and Douglas, whose absolutist reading of the First Amendment—"Congress shall make no law" means *no* law—was burdened with its own intellectual difficulties.

The debate over judicial review of McCarthyite legislation initially turned on two questions: whether the First Amendment occupied a "preferred position" in the constitutional scheme; and whether a "balancing test" that weighed national security interests against the interest in freedom of speech represented a legitimate application of the First Amendment.

By the time Brennan joined the Court in 1956, the differences between Frankfurter and Black had hardened. Before he was appointed, Frankfurter had often applauded the great civil liberties dissents delivered by his judicial heroes, Holmes and Brandeis. During the Cold War, however, Frankfurter increasingly ignored this heritage or else maintained that the Holmes-Brandeis dissents were inapplicable to a well-organized international Communist conspiracy.

Against Black's rigid absolutism, Frankfurter proposed a balancing test for resolving First Amendment issues. But the problem was that Frankfurter and his allies frequently defined the balance as one between the national security, on one hand, and the individual's right to speak on the other. Such a "category mistake," many commentators were quick to note, stacked the deck in favor of upholding all Cold War measures, for who could "balance" one individual's right to speak against the survival of the entire society? A proper balancing test needed to take into account the systemic damage that occurred every time the Court tolerated repression of civil liberties. As a result of this blatant misuse, the balancing test in civil liberties litigation deservedly acquired a bad reputation among liberal justices, and Warren Court opinions are filled with angry denunciations of its use. If it had been applied with more sensitivity and courage, the balancing test might actually have offered a more intellectually coherent methodology than Justice Black's dogmatic absolutism, which ultimately depended on an unrealistic "bright line" distinction between speech and action to escape absurdity.

Justice Brennan's great achievement was that he managed to reformulate completely the issues in First Amendment jurisprudence. Breaking out of the intellectual deadlock between Frankfurter and Black, he introduced four new concepts into the Court's analysis of free speech issues: the idea of "chilling effects"; the "void for vagueness" doctrine; the notion of an overbroad statute ("overbreadth"); and the legitimacy of a so-called facial challenge to statutes affecting First Amendment rights.

1. *Chilling Effects.* In his second term on the Court, Brennan

reformulated the reason why "[w]here the transcendent value of speech is involved" challenged statutes must receive strict scrutiny by the Court. In *Speiser* v. *Randall* (1958), he struck down a California loyalty oath that was made a precondition for a tax exemption on the ground that it put the burden of proof on the person seeking the exemption to swear that he was not disloyal. "The man who knows that he must bring forth proof and persuade another of the lawfulness of his conduct necessarily must steer far wider of the unlawful zone than if the State must bear these burdens," Brennan wrote.

In *NAACP* v. *Button* (1963), previously discussed, in which Virginia sought to put the NAACP out of business by invoking its statute barring lawyers from soliciting business, Brennan declared that First Amendment freedoms "need breathing space to survive." And in *New York Times Co.* v. *Sullivan* (1964), discussed at greater length in Chapter 3, involving a First Amendment challenge to Alabama's defamation law, he observed that under the Alabama law "would-be critics of official conduct may be deterred from voicing their criticism . . . because of doubt about whether it can be proved in court or fear of the expense of having to do so. They tend to make only statements which 'steer far wider of the unlawful zone.' "

The chilling-effects doctrine thus focused attention on the wider consequences of laws that suppressed speech. Statutes could now be challenged even when the particular application at issue might survive a First Amendment balancing test, since such statutes' mere presence on the books would tend to prevent others from exercising their First Amendment rights to the fullest extent. The chilling-effects doctrine was more than an important legal formula; it also reflected a deep understanding of what had actually happened in American society during the McCarthy Era. As we saw in Chapter 1, Brennan publicly deplored the excesses of the McCarthyite investigative committees. He recognized that Cold War witch-hunts not only unjustly persecuted many people but also led to the stagnation of American political, cultural, and intellectual life, as fear of being singled out and persecuted for strong or deviant opinions spread.

2. *Void for Vagueness.* The "void for vagueness" doctrine followed from Brennan's analysis of the chilling effects created by laws that interfere with free expression. If a statute is vague about the offense it is proscribing or about the persons it is meant to reach, individuals might refrain from legitimate speech out of fear that the statute might be construed against them. For that reason, Brennan wrote in *Button*, "it does not follow that the Court now has only a clear-cut task to decide whether the [defendant's] activities . . . are constitutionally privileged. If the line drawn . . . between the permitted and prohibited activities of the NAACP . . . is an ambiguous one," that is enough to invalidate it. "The objectionable quality of vagueness . . . does not depend upon absence of fair notice" to the defendant but rather on its chilling effect on the rest of society.

The "void for vagueness" doctrine reintroduced an old criminal law idea, but gave it a new spin. It had always been true that a criminal defendant could claim that he should not be punished under a law so vague that he had no notice in advance whether his conduct was criminal or not. Under the traditional view, however, if the trial court "construed" the words of the statute and gave it a clear meaning that unambiguously covered the defendant's conduct, then this "narrowing" interpretation saved the statute from constitutional challenge for vagueness.

Traditionally, a defendant could not successfully challenge a statute on the grounds that it could be unconstitutionally applied to other people. A defendant had no "standing" to raise the claims of others. If those other individuals wanted to challenge the statute, they could do so if they were indicted for violating it.

After Brennan redefined the evil of ambiguous statutes by focusing on their chilling effects, however, the void-for-vagueness doctrine was transformed. It was no longer primarily focused on the particular defendant and whether he had received adequate notice his behavior was criminal; instead, the focus had shifted to anonymous individuals who might have engaged in what Brennan called "self-censorship" out of fear that the vague statute might be applied to them.

To appreciate how widely accepted the void-for-vagueness doctrine became, let us turn to the majority opinion in *Baggett* v. *Bullitt* (1964) by Justice White, not otherwise known for his strong defense of civil liberties. The case challenged loyalty oaths for University of Washington teachers, who had been required to swear that they were not "subversive persons" or members of "subversive organizations." Following Justice Brennan's lead, and quoting from his opinion in *Speiser*, White held that the loyalty oaths were unconstitutionally vague because of their potential chilling effect on oath-takers, who were required to "steer far wide of the unlawful zone." "Those with a conscientious regard for what they solemnly swear or affirm, sensitive to the perils posed by the oath's indefinite language, avoid the risk of loss of employment, and perhaps profession, only by restricting their conduct to that which is unquestionably safe," White wrote. "Free speech may not be so inhibited."

3. *Overbreadth*. Brennan's deployment of the chilling-effects doctrine also drastically affected the treatment of challenges to "overbroad" laws. Under the traditional view, if a defendant was indicted under a statute that was "overbroad"—i.e., the law covered both conduct that was constitutionally protected and conduct that could constitutionally be punished—then the only question was whether this particular defendant's conduct could be punished under the Constitution. Again, a defendant had no standing to raise the constitutional claims of others.

But Brennan's reformulation permitted defendants to act as "private attorneys general," who could raise a claim on behalf of the public interest that overbroad statutes produced a "chilling effect" on society's free expression. As Brennan put it, in *NAACP* v. *Button*, "The objectionable quality of vagueness and overbreadth does not depend upon absence of fair notice to a criminally accused . . . but upon the danger of tolerating, in the area of First Amendment freedoms, the existence of a penal statute susceptible of sweeping and improper application."

We can observe a particularly dramatic application of the overbreadth doctrine in *United States* v. *Robel* (1967), previously discussed, involving a criminal prosecution against a member of the Communist Party who had knowingly worked in a defense facility in violation of the McCarran Act. Even though the trial court had limited the law's application to "active members" of Communist organizations, Chief Justice Warren held that it was still overbroad. The Court had previously said that active members could not be punished unless they had knowledge of the organization's illegal purposes; such proof was absent here. "It is precisely because [this] statute sweeps indiscriminately across all types of association with Communist-action groups, without regard to the quality and degree of membership, that it runs afoul of the First Amendment," Warren wrote. Even if Robel could constitutionally be punished, in short, he could successfully challenge the law because it might unconstitutionally be applied to others.

4. *"Facial" Challenge.* All of this meant that it was now possible to launch what is known as a "facial" challenge to vague and overbroad laws that interfered with free expression. It was not necessary to wait and see how these laws were actually applied; they could be held unconstitutional "on their face." Whereas, under the traditional view, the statute might be "saved" through a narrowing interpretation by a court, the chilling-effects analysis showed that such an interpretation would come too late in the process to undo the harm to free expression.

This point was especially important in cases involving Supreme Court review of statutes passed by Southern legislatures for the purpose of harassing or suppressing the civil rights movement. Under traditional doctrine, the Supreme Court was bound by a state high court's interpretation of its own laws. In addition, the Supreme Court was forced to rely on the state court's assessment of the facts in the particular case. The overbreadth doctrine, however, freed the Supreme Court from dependence on trial and appellate records developed by hostile Southern judges. It was no longer necessary to attempt to decide whether in the specific case, filtered through the findings of Southern judges, the particular defendant could be constitutionally punished. Rather, a law could be held unconstitutional and invalid on its face, freeing civil rights defendants from litigating many individual constitutional challenges.

V

The Evolving Concept of Democracy

One of the most important changes in Supreme Court jurisprudence during the Warren Era was the new central role of democracy. As constitutional law scholar John Hart Ely has suggested, in the Warren Era democracy became the fundamental ideal that gave meaning to the spirit of the Constitution.

For the Founding Fathers, democracy was a negative concept. Direct popular rule, without the "filter" of representative government, stirred intense fears of mob rule, of "tyranny of the majority." The Founders' ideal of republican government was thus very different from our modern understanding of democracy. True, it did include a commitment to popular consent, which represented a distinct improvement on European varieties of elite and hierarchical rule. All the Founders believed that at least one branch of the legislature should represent popular opinion and that the consent of the people, through their representatives, was an indispensable precondition for governmental legitimacy. But they certainly did not believe that the Senate or any second chamber of the legislature must also reflect popular opinion, or even that representative government in general was required to mirror the direct and unmediated opinions of the populace.

For the Framers, republican government did not even entail universal white male suffrage, let alone enfranchisement of all adult citizens. Though property qualifications for voting were rapidly eliminated for white males even before the Civil War—a major difference, let us remember, between the United States and most other Western societies—in most states women did not win the right to vote until the Nineteenth Amendment was ratified in 1920.

Before the Civil War, many states deprived even free blacks of the vote. Americans never dreamed that eventually four million former slaves and their descendants would also have a claim to participate in choosing a government. Even after the Fifteenth Amendment made it unconstitutional for states to refuse the vote on the basis of race, the reality in the South remained very different. One hundred years after the Civil War, the vast majority of Southern blacks continued to be disenfranchised. They attained the vote only after the Voting Rights Act of 1965, passed at the height of the civil rights movement, authorized federal intervention to force Southern states to register and protect black voters.

African Americans were not the only ones left without the franchise after the Civil War. The Fifteenth Amendment did not even apply to thousands of Chinese immigrants. Not until 1943 did Congress repeal the racist Chinese Exclusion Acts, which barred Chinese Americans from becoming American citizens; Congress did not declare that "the right to be or become a citizen shall not be abridged because of race" until 1952.

The Framers created many other barriers against popular rule. Only in 1913, with the passage of the Seventeenth Amendment, did popular election of the United States Senate replace election by state legislatures. Similarly, the Framers intended that the President would be chosen by an Electoral College composed of "notables" who would serve as another means of weakening the direct force of popular opinion. While the rapid development of a two-party system turned the Framers' idea of independent presidential electors into an anachronism, it was only during the second half of the twentieth century that widespread adoption of party primaries finally ended control by a small group of party bosses and elected officials over the selection of presidential candidates.

Democracy began to be applauded as a political ideal only with the emergence of Populism and Progressivism around the turn of the century. During this period many states, especially in the West, adopted the initiative and referendum, providing for a measure of direct popular rule. In the 1940s, democracy also began to be invoked more frequently as a fundamental ideal in the Supreme Court, amid increasingly intense efforts to distinguish democracy first from Nazism and then from Soviet totalitarianism. In constitutional history, arguments over the meaning of democracy were central to debates that split the New Deal majority on the Supreme Court almost immediately after it came to power in 1937.

The Carolene Products *Footnote* *and the Split in the New Deal Majority*

The New Deal justices appointed by President Franklin Delano Roosevelt all agreed on one point: that the so-called *Lochner* era of the Supreme Court was a disaster. Named after the notorious decision in *Lochner* v. *New York* (1905), which struck down a state law regulating maximum hours of work as a violation of the "due process" clause of the Fourteenth Amendment, the *Lochner* era came generally to symbolize the opposition of the Supreme Court to progressive social and economic reform legislation. In response, early-twentieth-century Progressive opponents of the *Lochner* Court developed various critiques of its assumptions, one of the most prominent of which was that the Court's decisions were hostile to the democratic will. They generalized this critique further to assert that judicial review of legislation by the Supreme Court was itself a contradiction of democratic principles and that only a policy of judicial restraint could avoid repeating the illegitimate practices of the *Lochner* Court.

Justice Felix Frankfurter, a New Deal appointee, became the

most famously unbending advocate of judicial restraint as "deference" to the will of the people expressed by the legislature. As we have seen, however, the same principle of deference that served Frankfurter as a bulwark against Lochnerian pro-business activism led him in later years to deny that there were constitutional problems with repressive, McCarthyite legislation. From the beginning, judicial "deference" was a double-edged sword. How could the principle of judicial restraint be reconciled with a commitment to civil liberties? This would prove to be one of the defining questions of the Warren Era.

One year after the triumph of the pro–New Deal majority in 1937, one of its members, Justice Harlan Fiske Stone, foreshadowed the future split among the justices by including a memorable footnote in an otherwise forgettable case. The case, *United States* v. *Carolene Products Co.*, involved governmental economic regulation similar to that in *Lochner*. The New Dealers had long urged the *Lochner* Court to exercise judicial restraint in reviewing such laws and defer to the policy judgments of democratically elected legislatures. Justice Stone agreed with this criticism. In the ordinary case of constitutional review of economic or social legislation, his footnote began, judicial restraint ought to be the rule, and the Supreme Court should defer to legislative policy judgments. But, he continued, there are three important exceptions to this presumption of judicial restraint. It may be necessary to exercise "more exacting judicial scrutiny" when reviewing (1) legislation that appears to violate one of the provisions of the Bill of Rights (the first ten amendments to the Constitution); (2) "legislation which restricts those political processes which can ordinarily be expected to bring about repeal of undesirable legislation"; or (3) "statutes directed at particular religions or national or racial minorities," because "prejudice against discrete and insular minorities may be a special condition, which tends seriously to curtail the operation of those political processes ordinarily to be relied upon to protect minorities . . ."

The *Carolene Products* footnote foreshadowed the split in the

New Deal majority between those, like Justice Frankfurter, who believed that democracy required across-the-board judicial restraint, and those justices who, following the spirit of Justice Stone's footnote, insisted that there should be stricter review of laws that interfere with the democratic process (such as laws restricting the First Amendment freedoms of speech and the press). The famous footnote was thus an important part of modern debates over the nature and meaning of democracy itself. Early-twentieth-century Progressives, with the goal of delegitimating the *Lochner* Court's resistance to popular reform, had presented a one-dimensional view of democracy as unrestrained majority rule. The Progressive advocacy of judicial restraint necessarily presumed that, by definition, judicial review was anti-democratic whenever it struck down laws that had been passed by legislative majorities.

The *Carolene Products* footnote sought to escape from the traditional Progressive conclusion that the exercise of judicial review was inherently undemocratic. Justice Stone aspired to develop a theory of judicial review that could be compatible with a commitment to democracy. As John Hart Ely has shown, it was Stone's modest-appearing footnote that laid the groundwork for much of the Warren Court's constitutional jurisprudence.

The Carolene Products *Footnote and the Warren Court*

In his book *Democracy and Distrust*, Ely argued that the Warren Court read the *Carolene Products* footnote as requiring judicial supervision of the constitutional framework of democracy. Following the logic of the footnote, the Warren Court recognized for the first time that the First Amendment rights of speech, the press, and association were entitled to a preferred position in a democratic system, since they were the very foundation of democracy itself. What has been less appreciated is the particular way in which the Court understood and put into practice Justice

Stone's third paragraph, acknowledging the need for especially strict constitutional scrutiny of laws aimed at "discrete and insular minorities." The Warren Court recognized not only that representation of minorities was an integral part of democracy but also that truly effective representation required that all people be guaranteed dignity and worth. The Court understood that democracy could not be treated as merely procedural but required attention to substantive values.

Brown v. *Board of Education* added a new and important dimension to the Warren Court's reading of the third paragraph of the *Carolene Products* footnote. Until that time, the footnote's three paragraphs were generally understood to have separate and distinct underlying purposes. The second paragraph, dealing with the democratic process, was understood to mean that the protection of First Amendment rights, for example, is a precondition for a functioning democracy. When a court strikes down a law interfering with freedom of speech, it does so for the purpose of enhancing, not opposing, democracy.

The third paragraph, however, was originally assumed to mean that discrete and insular minorities, being constantly threatened by the tyranny of the majority, are too weak to protect themselves within the democratic process. Only more active judicial review can regulate the conflict between majority rule and minority rights. The third paragraph was thus read to reiterate the Framers' original view that democracy constantly threatens minority rights and that the justification of judicial review was not that it perfected and protected democracy but rather that it tempered democracy's excesses.

We can grasp this idea more concretely by asking whether the *Brown* decision was consistent with democracy. It has often been said that by striking down racial segregation the Court was protecting the rights of blacks—surely, the clearest example in American history of "a discrete and insular minority"—from tyranny by the white majority. Indeed, if democracy means simply that the majority should always have its way, we would be forced to say that judicial review is anti-democratic, even when it strikes down laws establishing racial segregation.

But it is also possible to put the matter differently, and to argue that laws establishing or enforcing racial separation are themselves undemocratic; that democracy is incompatible with laws that create fundamental inequalities among a nation's citizens. For example, we would have no difficulty in understanding a statement that slavery is incompatible with democracy, or that until South Africa eliminated racial apartheid it could not be a democratic society. Similarly, we could easily understand the view that freedom of religion is essential to maintaining pluralistic values that provide the foundation for a democratic society. On this view, when a court strikes down laws oppressing a discrete and insular minority, it is acting not in opposition to but in support of democratic values.

This question about the scope and meaning of democratic theory began to come to the fore during the Warren Era.

The Warren Court—Redefining Democracy

It is important to understand that the Warren Court did not regard constitutional rights as in conflict with democracy but rather as constitutive of democracy. Much of the standard interpretation of the Warren Court depends on seeing it through a particular frame, what I would call the Federalist understanding. This notion assumes that the central dilemma of American constitutional law is how to reconcile a conflict between majority rule and minority rights and prevent a passionate majority from dominating minorities. The Federalist understanding is consistent with the Founders' fear of the tyranny of the majority.

In contemporary constitutional discussion, however, the Federalist understanding has developed into a cartoon in which democracy is defined as unfettered majority rule and judicial enforcement of constitutional rights is said to raise a "counter-majoritarian difficulty." Protection of minority rights is thus presented as a necessary interference with the workings of democracy. Such a simplistic definition of democracy is inadequate to understand the constitutional theory of the Warren Court. The Court's jurisprudence, as we have seen, relied on a reinterpretation of the third paragraph of the Carolene Products footnote that made protection of minority rights central to democracy. Moreover, the Court's focus on the centrality of minority rights redefined democracy itself, emphasizing equality of treatment as a necessary precondition for democracy.

To grasp the full impact of the Warren Court's redefinition of democracy, it is necessary to understand the wider context of twentieth-century debates over the meaning of democracy. The recent emergence of universal suffrage, combined with constitutional guarantees of fundamental rights, has produced an explosion of theories of democracy during the past half century. These theories are distributed along a continuum between two polar positions. At one end are minimalist theories that limit the requirements of democracy to free and fair elections with universal suffrage. Minimalist theories tend to focus on process values to the exclusion of substantive values. At the opposite pole, we find theories of democracy that focus on substantive values. These theories emphasize that unless there is political (or even social and economic) equality, there can be no real democratic system.

There is further debate at the substantive end of the spectrum between those who argue that the ideal of democracy requires only political equality—such as the right to an equally effective vote—and those who maintain that there can be no democracy —no effective political equality—without relative social and economic equality. If, for example, there are substantial differences of educational opportunity because of differences of wealth, then there can hardly be real political equality, since citizens will have widely different access to political knowledge and understanding, as well as leisure time in which to engage in politics. If elections are widely dependent on campaign contributions, the wealthy may have disproportionate influence over election results. If control of the media is based on wealth or political influence, then there can hardly be real political equality.

These examples are designed to demonstrate how difficult it is to define democracy as political equality without legitimately raising the question about whether it is possible to have real political equality amid substantial social and economic inequalities. This difficulty is perhaps the strongest argument for a "minimalist" definition of democracy that would ignore the substantive issue of equality. To the Warren Court, however, such a minimalist definition of democracy proved unsatisfactory. Instead, the Court attempted to give substantive content to democracy through its decisions privileging dignity and equality for all people. The Court developed its concept of democracy in important part in a series of decisions revolving around the value of substantive political equality—the Reapportionment Cases.

One Person, One Vote: The Reapportionment Cases

When asked after he had retired what his most important decision was, Earl Warren surprisingly answered: not *Brown* v. *Board of Education*, as might have been expected, but the Reapportionment Cases. Only an understanding of the democratic values that lay at the foundation of Warren's decisions can explain such an unexpected response. When the Supreme Court was asked to hear challenges to the fairness of state legislative apportionment in *Baker* v. *Carr* (1962), the maldistribution of legislative districts had become a national disgrace. As the shift in population from rural to urban areas accelerated during the twentieth century, entrenched state legislators simply refused to redraw election districts to reflect population changes. In Tennessee, the state whose legislative apportionment was under attack in *Baker*, legislators had for sixty years ignored a state constitutional requirement that they reapportion every decade. In the lower house of

Tennessee's two-house legislature, election districts were drawn so that less than 40 percent of the population could elect a majority of representatives.

The situation was much worse in other states. In eleven state senates, a voting majority could be elected by less than 20 percent of the population, including California (10.7 percent), Florida (14.1 percent), and Nevada (8 percent). In only seventeen states was as much as 40 percent of the population required for majority control. In lower houses, there were four states in which potential majority control was in the hands of fewer than 20 percent of the voters, while only seventeen required at least 40 percent for such control.

As a result, state legislatures, dominated by rural interests, regularly refused to vote cities a fair share of tax revenues. This was even more true if we consider that cities were in greater need, since the poor and underprivileged—those especially dependent upon governmental services—tended to be concentrated in urban centers. Nor was it lost on the Warren Court justices in the aftermath of *Brown* that since World War II there had been a major migration of black citizens from Southern rural areas to the large urban industrial centers of the Northeast and Midwest. Legislative malapportionment served as another device for diluting the political power of urban black voters.

In a great scholarly opinion by Justice Brennan, the Supreme Court in *Baker* v. *Carr* held that a challenge to legislative apportionment was not a "political question" that the Court should refuse to entertain. *Baker* did not itself rule on the question of whether Tennessee's unequally apportioned districts were unconstitutional. It did hold that the question was "justiciable," opening the door for future lawsuits that might overturn such unequal districts. Brennan's opinion constituted a dramatic overruling of an earlier decision, *Colegrove* v. *Green* (1949), written by Justice Felix Frankfurter, who had been Brennan's teacher at Harvard Law School. One month after delivering his bitter dissent in *Baker*, Frankfurter suffered a stroke and shortly there-

after retired from the Court. The appointment of Arthur Goldberg to succeed Frankfurter produced the most important shift
in the balance of power on the Warren Court, leading some
historians to treat the Warren Era as divided into two distinct
periods.

One of the great themes of the Warren Era is the Court's shift
away from the philosophy of judicial restraint espoused by Justice
Frankfurter. The decision in *Baker* v. *Carr* was a dramatic signal
that Frankfurter's influence was on the wane. Even more important, perhaps, by the time Frankfurter left the Court his once
dominant philosophy of across-the-board judicial restraint, denying even a "preferred position" to freedom of speech, was in
the process of being rejected, as the Court moved cautiously
against substantial Cold War remnants of McCarthyism. And, as
we shall see, the move away from Frankfurter's influence also
had dramatic consequences for the Warren Court's decisions in
criminal cases, which include some of the decisions for which the
Court is best known, and which continue to have the greatest
effects on us today.

The Reapportionment Cases, however, were perhaps the most
dramatic example of the change that Frankfurter's retirement
and Goldberg's appointment, which first created a liberal majority, brought to the Court. In *Reynolds* v. *Sims* (1964), Chief Justice
Warren first applied the "one person, one vote" rule governing
apportionment of congressional legislative districts to *state* legislatures. The decision was a dramatic reinterpretation of the
Fourteenth Amendment's Equal Protection Clause, and a fulfill-
ment of the promise of *Baker* v. *Carr*. The Reapportionment
Cases produced some of the most far-reaching opinions delivered
by the Warren Court, underlining the recent emergence of democracy as the foundational value of Warren Court constitutional jurisprudence.

After *Baker* v. *Carr* had ruled that the Court had the power to
hear challenges to unequal legislative apportionment, few observers had imagined that, in the end, the Court would hold that

the Equal Protection Clause required the same rule of equal districting for both houses of state legislatures. After all, one only needed to look to the United States Senate, with its two Senators per state regardless of population, to see that the upper house in American constitutional theory was originally designed to emulate the aristocratic British House of Lords, rather than to be a mirror of popular opinion. True, original constitutional theory did suppose that the lower house of the legislature should more or less reflect the distribution of the popular vote. Yet, even that ideal, we have seen, had been regularly flouted by entrenched rural state legislators. Still, the idea that equal protection meant that legislative districts in both houses should be required to contain equal populations was a dramatic rejection of the original constitutional understanding. It could only be justified on the grounds that democracy—the right to an equally effective vote —had evolved to become the foundational constitutional ideal. Such a view presupposed a "living Constitution," one that, in Chief Justice Marshall's words, changed and evolved over time, adapting to "the various crises of human affairs." Under such a view, the Court could legitimately generate new fundamental constitutional meanings.

The Division over the Idea of a Living Constitution

As we have seen, the question of a "living Constitution" was a recurring theme in Warren Court jurisprudence. At the very outset of the Warren Era, *Brown v. Board of Education* itself raised the question of whether constitutional meaning changes over time. After the first argument in *Brown*, Justice Frankfurter called for reargument to examine whether racial segregation was barred under the original understanding of the Fourteenth Amendment. His law clerk, future Yale law professor Alexander M. Bickel, wrote a memorandum to Frankfurter which he eventually published as "The Original Understanding and the Segregation Decision." After elaborate historical research, Bickel concluded that the Framers of the Fourteenth Amendment had no specific intent to abolish racially segregated schooling. A rigid adherence to the original intent of the Framers would thus preclude interpreting the Equal Protection Clause to bar segregation. But, Bickel insisted, that conclusion should not end the search for the meaning of the Equal Protection Clause. Since the Framers chose to write the Amendment in general terms, he maintained, later generations should not be bound by the particular way the Framers would have applied the general language of the Equal Protection Clause at the time it was adopted and ratified. The meaning of general language like "equal protection of the laws" can depend only on its specific application in changing historical circumstances. This "changing circumstances" interpretation of the Fourteenth Amendment was incorporated into Chief Justice Warren's opinion in *Brown*.

The question of a "living Constitution" once again came to a head in *Harper* v. *Virginia State Board of Elections* (1966), in which Justice Douglas wrote a majority opinion declaring that Virginia's poll tax violated the Equal Protection Clause. Using the most provocative language possible, Douglas argued that the changing meaning of equal protection justified reversing a thirty-year-old decision that had upheld a state poll tax. "[T]he Equal Protection Clause," Douglas wrote, "is not shackled to the political theory of a particular era. In determining what lines are unconstitutionally discriminatory, we have never been confined to historic notions of equality . . ." And he cited *Brown* v. *Board of Education* as justification for saying that the meaning of equality changes with changing circumstances.

Douglas's opinion provoked a bitter dissent from Justice Black. "I did not vote to hold segregation in public schools unconstitutional on any such theory," Black wrote, pointedly separating himself from his closest ally for almost three decades. "I thought when *Brown* was written, and I think now, that Mr. Justice Harlan was correct in 1896 when he dissented from *Plessy v. Ferguson* . . . I did not join the opinion of the Court in *Brown* on any theory that segregation . . . denied equal protection in 1954 but did not similarly deny it in 1868 . . ." Douglas had also cited the "one person, one vote" decision in *Reynolds* v. *Sims* for his proposition that the meaning of equal protection changes over time. Black had concurred in that decision. It is difficult to see how Black could possibly have denied Douglas's suggestion that the original understanding of the Equal Protection Clause did not require both houses of a state legislature to be apportioned according to population. It seems clear that any such conclusion could be based only on historically changing ideas about equality and democracy.

Brown and *Harper* highlight the problematic nature of a strictly originalist theory of constitutional interpretation, and its inadequacy for adjudicating twentieth-century constitutional issues. Attempting to resolve questions of interpretation by deferring to the intentions of the Framers of the Constitution leads to several practical and philosophical difficulties. First, the Fourteenth Amendment, for example, was not written by one person but was arrived at through a process of debate, politicking, and compromise. It may be that the various participants in that process had different intentions about what the amendment should mean and how it should be implemented; those intentions may even have been contradictory. Moreover, some would argue that even if the Constitution had one author with one coherent intention as to its meaning and future implementation, that intention could never be completely accessible to judges, or even historians, two centuries later. Finally, assuming for the sake of argument that the Constitution's Framers did have a unitary, discoverable intention as to how it should be implemented in a particular case, it is not clear that that intention should necessarily govern constitutional interpretation in the late twentieth century, a profoundly different time and society from that of the Framers. The Constitution endures because it is a vehicle for the most central values of American society; but those values necessarily evolve as society changes. However acceptable school segregation may have seemed to the drafters of the Fourteenth Amendment, our evolving understanding of the larger principles embodied in that amendment made it completely unacceptable by 1954.

Positive Liberty

The Warren Court once again faced the challenge of interpreting an eighteenth-century Constitution in twentieth-century America in a series of cases challenging the constitutionality of the administration of New Deal entitlement programs.

One of the eighteenth-century ideas that informed the Constitution and its Framers was that liberty is only a *negative* concept involving freedom *from* external constraint. By contrast, the post–World War II social democratic European constitutions guaranteeing welfare and employment rights were inspired by a *positive* view of liberty that regarded government as having an affirmative obligation to promote the conditions for maximum individual self-fulfillment.

Early in the twentieth century, Progressive thinkers in Britain and America began to question the dogmas of nineteenth-century laissez-faire liberalism. Led by the philosophers Thomas Hill Green in England and John Dewey in America, they challenged the twin ideas that liberty is measured by the absence of external constraint and that liberty is increased by reducing the role of government. Most New Deal liberals believed that expanded government could increase the opportunities for human self-development by creating a safety net that would protect vulnerable individuals against the unpredictability of the free market.

Nineteenth-century legal liberals drew a sharp distinction between government benefits and private property. A welfare grant was thought to be a "privilege" bestowed by the grace of government, not a "property right." Since a privilege need not have been granted in the first place, the government could revoke it in any manner and for any reason it wished. But the emergence in the twentieth century of the welfare state and its associated "entitlements" blurred the boundary between rights and privileges; New Deal entitlements did not fit easily into either category. During its last years, the Warren Court began to challenge both the negative conception of liberty and the bright-line distinction between rights and privileges. Slowly and incompletely, the Warren Court moved toward the social democratic view that the state has a positive duty to provide its citizens with the conditions for individual self-development.

In both its due process and equal protection jurisprudence, the Warren Court began to incorporate some version of the social democratic vision. In a notable series of decisions beginning with *Speiser* v. *Randall* (1958) and culminating in *Shapiro* v. *Thompson* (1969) and *Goldberg* v. *Kelly* (1970), Justice Brennan indicated an awareness that the emergence of the welfare state required a substantial reconsideration of the traditional legal distinction between a right and a privilege. *Speiser* struck down an unconstitutional loyalty oath that had been made a precondition for receiving a state tax exemption. For Brennan, an unconstitutional precondition could not be attached to a government benefit just because it was labeled a "privilege."

In one of his famous opinions, *Goldberg* v. *Kelly*, Brennan carried the collapse of the right–privilege distinction still further. Declaring that welfare benefits were a form of property that could not be taken away without a hearing, he refused to accept the traditional definition of welfare as a privilege gratuitously conferred by the state. *Goldberg* was a landmark case that expanded our understanding of due process and of the relationship between the state and the individual. In a speech given much later, Brennan explained his vision of due process:

Due process asks whether government has treated someone fairly, whether individual dignity has been honored, whether the worth of an individual has been acknowledged. If due process values are to be preserved in the bureaucratic state of the late twentieth century, it may be essential that officials possess passion . . . that understands the pulse of life beneath the official version of events. [The decision in *Goldberg*] can be seen as injecting passion into a system whose abstract rationality had led it astray.

In a second major area, equal protection, the Warren Court led conservatives to fear that it was intent on turning wealth into a "suspect" class for purposes of equal protection litigation. In cases such as *Griffin* v. *Illinois* (1956) and *Douglas* v. *California* (1963), the Court held that the Equal Protection Clause required that access to the courts not be precluded by poverty. In *Griffin*, Justice Black struck down a law that required poor criminal defendants to pay for trial transcripts before they could appeal their convictions; in *Douglas*, Justice Douglas ruled that criminal defendants who want to appeal their convictions are entitled to the assistance of counsel. "[T]here can be no equal justice," wrote Douglas, "where the kind of an appeal a man enjoys depends on the amount of money he has."

In *Shapiro* v. *Thompson* (1969), Justice Brennan relied on the Equal Protection Clause to hold unconstitutional various state laws establishing "waiting periods" before new residents could receive welfare aid. In his dissent, Justice Harlan expressed conservatives' concern that in *Shapiro* Brennan had "applied an equal protection doctrine of relatively recent vintage." Though Harlan accepted the idea that any racial classification by the states was "suspect" under the Equal Protection Clause, he worried that the liberal majority's "recent extensions" of equal protection beyond race meant that any classification based on ability to pay was also suspect. "I do not consider wealth a 'suspect' . . . criterion," Harlan declared.

Harlan surely overstated the principle underlying the Warren Court's extensions of equal protection. There was still a long way to go before these Warren Court decisions could be generally characterized as making wealth a "suspect" category. *Grif-*

fin and *Douglas* dealt with equal access to the judicial system, a long way from any general state obligation to provide equality. Similarly, the welfare residency requirement in *Shapiro* was struck down only because it abridged the fundamental constitutional right to travel; without the right to travel, there would have been no finding that the residency requirement was unconstitutional under the Equal Protection Clause.

Nevertheless, in these decisions the Warren Court did take the first steps toward elaborating a vision of "positive liberty" that would accord with its evolving conception of democracy as requiring both political and substantive equality. And Justice Brennan's infusion of passion into due process jurisprudence was not confined to welfare law but was echoed in the criminal law decisions of the Warren Court.

Incorporation of the Bill of Rights and the Warren Court's Criminal Justice Decisions

Most Americans are surprised to learn that, for most of American history, the Bill of Rights—the first ten amendments to the Constitution—did not apply to the states. This means that until quite recently a state was not constitutionally barred from abridging First Amendment rights of freedom of speech, press, or religion, unless there was a similar provision in the state's own constitution. In addition, before the Warren Court, the federal constitutional guaranties to criminal defendants of a right to counsel and protection against self-incrimination and unreasonable searches and seizures were not extended to state criminal trials.

There is little disagreement that the Framers of the original Constitution, fearing the powers of a newly established central government, drafted the Bill of Rights in order to restrict national, not state, power. Until the ratification of the Fourteenth Amendment (1868), no one really doubted that the Bill of Rights applied only to the federal government. But the passage of the

Fourteenth Amendment eventually generated a controversy over whether the Due Process Clause ("nor shall any State deprive any person of life, liberty, or property, without due process of law") was meant to incorporate the specific rights contained in the first ten amendments.

During the 1940s and 1950s, Justices Frankfurter and Black propounded two opposing views of the incorporation problem. Black, the Constitutional literalist, believed that every protection afforded by the Bill of Rights—no more and no less—was incorporated into the Fourteenth Amendment's Due Process Clause. Frankfurter, on the other hand, maintained that the Due Process Clause must be interpreted independently of the Bill of Rights, as a guarantee of "the immutable principles of justice as conceived by a civilized society." Because such "immutable principles" were thought to be few and far between, Frankfurter's position limited the efficacy of the Due Process Clause as a restriction on state power.

The dispute came to a head in *Adamson* v. *California* (1947), in which the Court was asked to decide whether a state criminal defendant's failure to testify could be held against him by a jury—a procedure that would not be allowed in federal court under the Fifth Amendment's protection against self-incrimination. Upholding Adamson's murder conviction by a 5–4 vote, the Court also upheld Justice Frankfurter's view of the Due Process Clause over an impassioned dissent by Black, who termed Frankfurter's position "an incongruous excrescence on our Constitution." After *Adamson*, Black continued to contend for his interpretation of the Constitution, with eventual success. One of the great revolutions of the Warren Court era was the shift from the dominance of the Frankfurter interpretation of due process to a majority position much closer in spirit to Justice Black's.

In *Mapp* v. *Ohio* (1961), the Court took the rare step of explicitly overruling an earlier Court decision. In *Wolf* v. *Colorado* (1949), Justice Frankfurter had held that the Due Process Clause does not mandate adoption by the states of the federal rule that evidence obtained by unreasonable searches and seizures, in violation of the Fourth Amendment, must be excluded at trial. In overturning *Wolf* and ruling that the exclusionary rule must also apply to the states, the *Mapp* Court took a major step away from Frankfurter's reading of the Due Process Clause.

In the years following *Mapp*, the Warren Court continued to expand the range of due process protections available to state criminal defendants. In *Robinson* v. *California* (1962), the Court ruled that the Eighth Amendment's protection against cruel and unusual punishment applied to the states. Subsequent cases extended to state criminal defendants the Fifth Amendment right against compelled self-incrimination (*Malloy* v. *Hogan* [1964]); the Sixth Amendment right to confront opposing witnesses (*Pointer* v. *Texas* [1965]); and the Sixth Amendment right to a speedy trial (*Klopfer* v. *North Carolina* [1967]), among others.

Perhaps the most significant of the line of post-*Mapp* decisions expanding due process protections was *Gideon* v. *Wainwright* (1963). After a state trial judge refused to appoint a lawyer to defend him, Clarence Gideon was convicted of breaking and entering a Florida pool hall. His conviction was affirmed on appeal, and Gideon sent a handwritten petition to the Supreme Court claiming that he had been deprived of due process at his trial. The Court decided to hear Gideon's case and appointed future justice Abe Fortas to represent him. Justice Black led a unanimous Court in overturning Gideon's conviction, holding that the Fourteenth Amendment guarantee of due process must incorporate the right of indigent criminal defendants to have counsel appointed for them under the Sixth Amendment. *Gideon* was a turning point in Fourteenth Amendment due process jurisprudence, and also a personal triumph for Black. In the 1942 case of *Betts* v. *Brady*, the Court had rejected his argument that the right to counsel should apply in all serious state criminal cases. Twenty-one years later, in *Gideon*, Black was able to overturn *Betts* with the support of all eight of his fellow justices. "I never thought I'd live to see [*Betts*] overruled," he said. *Gideon* was a high point in Black's long career on the Court.

In order to get nine votes for his opinion in *Gideon*, however, Black was forced to moderate his position that the Fourteenth Amendment required total incorporation of all provisions of the Bill of Rights. Instead, he based his opinion in *Gideon* on the idea that the right to counsel is "fundamental and essential to a fair trial" and is thus applicable to the states through the Fourteenth Amendment. Though he did not use the phrase, Black was adopting the doctrine of "selective incorporation," which held that the guarantees of the Bill of Rights that were fundamental to our justice system should be applied against the states just as they applied against the federal government. Justice Brennan had advocated selective incorporation as a middle position between incorporating the entire Bill of Rights into the Fourteenth Amendment and interpreting the Fourteenth Amendment as entirely independent of the Bill of Rights. When Black adopted Brennan's position in *Gideon*, he set the tone for the Warren Court's subsequent Fourteenth Amendment due process jurisprudence. In a later opinion he commented, "I believe as strongly as ever that the Fourteenth Amendment was intended to make the Bill of Rights applicable to the states. I have been willing to support the selective incorporation doctrine, however, as an alternative, [since it has] already worked to make most of the Bill of Rights' protections applicable to the States." It was a pragmatic decision. Though Black's "total incorporation" position never commanded a majority, the Warren Court's selective incorporation decisions, as they accumulated, came ever closer to the effective equivalent of total incorporation. Justice Frankfurter's restrictive vision of due process was emphatically rejected.

Because public debate has centered on the merits of such controversial decisions as *Miranda* v. *Arizona* (1966), requiring police officers to warn suspects of their rights, people have tended to overlook the vast constitutional revolution that the Warren Court criminal decisions represented. By extending most of the protections of the Bill of Rights to the states, the Supreme Court under Earl Warren was the first to insist upon uniform, national constitutional standards for judging the fairness of a state's criminal procedures. It was another expression of a long-term shift toward a more nationalized and centralized constitutional system that began to take shape as a result of the Civil War.

Of all the rulings of the Warren Court, none was more unpopular than its criminal justice decisions. *Miranda* v. *Arizona* in particular produced a storm of opposition. *Miranda* excluded confessions obtained by police from defendants who were not warned of their rights to remain silent and have counsel present during questioning. In a period of rising crime rates as well as increased civil disobedience deriving from both the civil rights and antiwar movements, public opinion supported Richard M. Nixon's 1968 campaign criticism of the Supreme Court for preferring the "criminal forces" over the "peace forces."

Chief Justice Warren seemed to have taken notice of the growing public opposition to the Warren Court's criminal decisions. In *Terry* v. *Ohio* (1968), the Chief Justice wrote a decision upholding a police "stop and frisk" that seemed, in effect, to allow police officers to evade the constitutional requirement that a suspect could not be searched without "probable cause" that a crime had been committed. Some Warren Court supporters see *Terry* as marking the effective end of Warren Court reform of the criminal justice system. "[W]hen we speak of the Warren Court's 'revolution' in American criminal procedure," Professor Yale Kamisar has observed, "we mean the Warren Court that lasted from 1961 (when the landmark case of *Mapp* v. *Ohio* was decided) to 1966 or 1967. In its final years, the Warren Court was not the same Court that had handed down *Mapp* or *Miranda*.

"The last years of the Warren Court constituted a period of social upheaval marked by urban riots, disorders on college campuses, ever-soaring crime statistics, ever-spreading fears of the breakdown of public order, and assassinations and near-assassinations of public figures." Strong criticism of the Court by many members of Congress and presidential candidate Richard Nixon resulted in "obviously retaliatory" anti-crime legislation that "contributed further to an atmosphere that was unfavorable to the continued vitality of the Warren Court's mission in criminal cases."

Did the Warren Court criminal justice decisions have any real effect on the behavior of the police? Some have suggested that the criminal justice decisions were a failure. It has been argued that while some Supreme Court decisions have resulted in allowing concededly guilty defendants to go free, there has been no demonstrable beneficial change in police practices. Some suggest that the police will always find their own ways to evade constitutional rules; others maintain that even in the best of circumstances the Supreme Court is just too distant from the day-to-day decisions of the policeman on the beat or in the station house to have any systematic effect on police behavior.

Yet we have come gradually to recognize that the culture of police departments varies widely, depending on whether there is organizational leadership as well as serious training and education of recruits in the values of civil liberties. This certainly suggests that different institutional practices and values can produce widely different organizational attitudes toward obeying the law.

If we ask whether the culture of the police station has changed since the Warren Court, the answer appears to be positive. Before the Warren Court, several generations of official commissions had documented and condemned the widespread brutality toward criminal suspects that had become standard operating procedure in many police departments. Confessions were regularly extracted with the help of the rubber hose or worse. In the South, there had been a long history of railroading black defendants into coerced confessions. In *Brown* v. *Mississippi* (1936), to take a horrific example, the Supreme Court unanimously overturned the conviction of three black defendants on the ground that their "confessions" had been coerced. The defendants had been tortured into confessing to murder and then convicted and sentenced to death in a one-day trial with no other evidence offered against them—the epitome of a "legal lynching."

In addition, in many cases state criminal defendants, particularly blacks, received little or no effective representation at trial. In *Powell* v. *Alabama* (1932), the first of the infamous "Scottsboro" cases to come before the Supreme Court, the Court overturned the convictions of eight young black men who had been accused of raping two white women while all were "riding the rails" on a freight train. The "Scottsboro Boys," as they came to be called, had been convicted and sentenced to death after attorneys appointed for them by the Alabama court did no investigation of the case and consulted with the defendants for only half an hour before the trials. The expansion of due process protection of state criminal defendants during the Warren years must be seen as a response to the long-standing abuse of due process epitomized by cases like *Brown* and *Powell*.

The point is that the success or failure of the Warren Court criminal cases ought to be measured in the long run by whether they have contributed to shaping a culture of civil liberties within police departments and the offices of public prosecutors. That such a culture could be initially created only by an "exclusionary rule," barring the use of evidence against the defendants, meant that sometimes a guilty defendant went free only because the police bungled. In cases of unconstitutional searches, the exclusionary rule was designed to deter the police by throwing out any conviction that was based on evidence that was obtained in an illegal search. But the downside of the exclusionary rule was that it also meant depriving juries of reliable evidence of the defendant's guilt.

The issue was different in the confession cases because the purpose of the *Miranda* rule was not only to affect police practices but also to exclude confessions that might have been unreliable because the police had been coercive. In the absence of any effective way of determining in each case whether the police had used improper means to obtain a confession, it seemed better to establish a uniform system that warned suspects of their right to remain silent.

Just as the Reapportionment Cases changed the structure of American democracy, the Warren Court's criminal justice decisions focused attention on the culture of police departments across the country. The criminal cases provide further evidence that the Warren Court viewed the protection of the rights of unpopular minorities as integral to democracy itself.

VI

Democratic Culture

The Reapportionment Cases showed that the Warren Court took democracy seriously as a constitutional ideal. Its decisions involving freedom of expression show the Court trying to make democracy a practical reality. The free speech cases allowed the Court to formulate the necessary conditions for achieving popular self-government through the ballot box. Beyond free and equal voting, there needed to be "uninhibited, robust, and wide-open" debate on public issues that would "assure unfettered interchange of ideas for the bringing about of political and social changes desired by the people." More than any Supreme Court in American history, the Warren Court was seriously attentive to the political culture that underlay democracy.

What is still more amazing is that the Warren Court did not limit its understanding of the preconditions for democracy to the narrowly political. It was the first Court to realize that there was a close connection between democratic political institutions and culture; that, indeed, there was such a thing as democratic *culture.*

Perhaps the best place to see this development is through the Court's decisions involving obscenity and the right to privacy. The story begins with the decision in *Roth* v. *United States* (1957), written by Justice Brennan in his first term on the Court. Holding that obscenity is not protected by the First Amendment, *Roth* nevertheless offered the most permissive definition of obscenity ever proposed until that time by any court. Material was not obscene unless it was "utterly without redeeming social importance." "All ideas having even the slightest redeeming social importance," Brennan wrote, "—unorthodox ideas, controversial ideas, even ideas hateful to the prevailing climate of opinion— have the full protection" of the First Amendment.

"[S]ex and obscenity are not synonymous," Brennan declared, in the midst of a decade known for its postwar resurgence of puritanism and its determination to censor movies and prevent Americans from reading books such as D. H. Lawrence's 1928 novel *Lady Chatterley's Lover* or Henry Miller's long-suppressed *Tropic of Cancer*. "Obscene material is material which deals with sex in a manner appealing to prurient interest," he announced.

> The portrayal of sex, e.g., in art, literature and scientific works, is not itself sufficient reason to deny material the constitutional protection of freedom of speech and press. Sex, a great and mysterious motive force in human life, has indisputably been a subject of absorbing interest to mankind through the ages; it is one of the vital problems of human interest and public concern.

The test for whether material is obscene, Brennan announced, is whether "to the *average* person, applying contemporary community standards, the *dominant* theme of the material *taken as a whole* appeals to the prurient interest [emphasis added]."

In light of the enormous changes that have taken place in American law and culture in the four decades since Brennan delivered his *Roth* opinion, it is easy to underestimate both the importance and the wisdom of his brilliant formulation. Only by locating *Roth* in its historical context can we avoid being unhistorical in our appreciation of its significance.

When *Roth* was brought before the Supreme Court, a respectable body of opinion, led by the distinguished civil libertarian Alexander Meiklejohn, sought to restrict the scope of free speech protections to "political" speech on the grounds that the First

Amendment was limited to fostering democratic politics. The Meikeljohn thesis thus drew a sharp distinction between political and cultural forms of expression. *Roth* was among the first Supreme Court opinions to reject this distinction and to acknowledge the relationship between culture and politics.

Justices Black and Douglas dissented in *Roth* on the "absolutist" ground that the First Amendment bars all restrictions on speech, even obscene speech. None of the rest of the justices, including Brennan, was ever willing to accept that proposition. Whatever one may say in defense of the Black-Douglas position, it is important not to forget that, in *Roth*, Brennan was able to assemble a majority behind a constitutional formula that was more protective of artistic expression than any that had been previously proposed.

By the time the Warren Court ended, however, Brennan's *Roth* formula had unraveled, as the difficult task of applying its various elements to a society undergoing unprecedented changes in sexual mores became increasingly evident. By 1964, it had already become apparent that Brennan had failed to rally a majority around a coherent and consistent application of his *Roth* formula. In *Jacobellis* v. *Ohio* (1964), a splintered Court produced seven different opinions, including Justice Stewart's memorable pronouncement about hardcore pornography: "I know it when I see it."

The justices divided over such questions as how to define "community" in *Roth*'s phrase "contemporary community standards"—e.g., whether there should be a national or local test of obscenity. A local test would mean that more straitlaced communities would be given greater leeway to suppress books and magazines, movies, theatrical productions, paintings, and other forms of artistic expression. A national standard would mean that uniform criteria would prevail throughout the United States, which in practice would mean that the more cosmopolitan assumptions of the cultural elite would be applied. In a period when television, dominated by national networks, was emerging as the leading influence over popular culture, the question might already have become moot.

Another problem that emerged with Brennan's formulation was whether the phrase "utterly without redeeming social value" incorporated unconscious prejudices in favor of "highbrow," as opposed to "lowbrow," culture. Shortly before *Jacobellis* came before the Court, Brennan drafted a memorandum to his colleagues that set out his main views on pornography. "The basic point of this memorandum," he concluded, "is that no bona fide work of art or information may be suppressed in the name of obscenity, even if it is deeply repulsive to the dominant current thought of the community." This view, critics noted, led the Court to embark on a misleading search for artistic merit from the vantage point of "highbrow" culture. In a period in which some of the most creative cultural achievements—such as the music of the Beatles—were directed at a mass audience, Justice Brennan's search for bona fide works of art left the impression that he was concerned only with protecting works such as the sixteenth-century painter Titian's nudes from the scorn of the philistines.

The truth is that in 1957 the Supreme Court justices were totally unprepared for the sexual revolution that was about to burst on the scene and thoroughly transform the most intimate aspects of American life. Themselves the products of a puritanical middle-class culture, the justices were surprised by the emergence of sexuality into mainstream popular culture that began in the 1950s with the Kinsey Reports on male and female sexuality of 1948 and 1953, the appearance of *Playboy* in 1953, and such scandalous best-selling novels as *Peyton Place* (1956). And if the justices were unprepared for the increased frankness of the 1950s, still less were they prepared for the developments of the 1960s and 1970s. Indeed, with the emergence of an increasingly self-confident gay culture, celebrating homosexuality through books and magazines, Justice Brennan's well-meant effort to define obscenity in terms of material that "appeals to the prurient interest" itself came to seem positively puritanical.

The shift to the Burger Court after 1969 produced decisions that sought to narrow Brennan's standard. In turn, Brennan grew more and more skeptical about whether any satisfactory formula would work, eventually rejecting his own approach in *Roth*. His dissent in a pornographic film case, *Paris Adult Theatre* I (1973), announced his new position:

> I am forced to conclude that the concept of "obscenity" cannot be defined with sufficient specificity and clarity to provide fair notice to persons who create and distribute sexually oriented materials, to prevent substantial erosion of protected speech as a byproduct of the attempt to suppress unprotected speech, and to avoid very costly institutional harms.

In a 1986 interview, Brennan acknowledged that the Court's failure to find "a solution to the definitional horror of obscenity" was one of his major "disappointments" on the Court and that maybe "it has been my fault." Still later, he confided that he had "put sixteen years into that damn obscenity thing . . . I tried and I tried, and I waffled back and forth, and I finally gave up." Perhaps Brennan's concession demonstrates that Justices Black and Douglas were right all along, and that their absolutist position on obscenity had anticipated the impossibility of reaching a consensus on a question that was in the midst of such dynamic cultural change.

One element of this dynamic cultural change that totally shifted the ground of the debate over pornography was the emergence of the feminist movement soon after the Warren Court had come to a close. The writings of Catharine MacKinnon and Andrea Dworkin made it painfully clear that much pornography was addressed to male fantasies about the degradation of women by men. Suddenly there was a split in the progressive, cosmopolitan coalition over the question of pornography, as some feminists called for greater regulation of hardcore pornography on the grounds that it created a culture harmful to women. Equally important, there was a serious debate over the effects of culture on action—on the effects of cultural images and symbols on the behavior of men toward women—a debate that did not necessarily carry the ancient baggage of puritan discomfort with sexuality.

In the end, it would be mistaken to dismiss the Court's efforts to deal with the constitutionality of obscenity as a failure. It may have been naïve to believe that any legal formula could adequately capture the values affecting so complex a subject, especially in a period of such dynamic social change. Yet, as in so many other areas of constitutional law, the Supreme Court did manage to create an educational dialogue about fundamental values that no other institution was capable of producing. By the time the Warren Court ended, there was no longer any substantial body of opinion that sought to exclude artistic expression from First Amendment protection by sharply distinguishing the political from the literary or cultural realms. In the midst of the social and cultural upheaval of the sixties, it was no longer possible to suppose that cultural expression has no effect on political action. But this also meant that one of the central organizing ideas of First Amendment jurisprudence—positing a sharp distinction between speech and action—began to collapse.

Symbolic Speech

The "sit-ins" against segregated public facilities in the early 1960s first raised the question of whether it was possible to distinguish between speech and action. But it was the "symbolic" protests against America's growing involvement in the war in Vietnam that challenged the very foundations of the speech-action distinction.

The distinction was especially important for Justice Black's absolutist view of the First Amendment. Once something was categorized as speech, Black insisted that no state interest, however compelling, could justify its suppression. Thus, as we have seen, Black rejected any use of a "balancing test" to decide First Amendment questions. Instead, he relied on a bright-line distinction between speech, which could never constitutionally be punished, and action, which could be. If one had asked Justice Black whether the state could punish a person for falsely shouting "Fire" in a crowded theater, he would have replied that it was not speech but action that was being punished.

Three "symbolic speech" cases involving antiwar protests strained the speech-action distinction to the breaking point. In *United States* v. *O'Brien* (1968), Chief Justice Warren relied on the distinction to uphold the conviction of Vietnam War protesters for burning their draft registration cards. "When 'speech' and 'nonspeech' elements are combined in the same course of conduct, a sufficiently important governmental interest in regulating the nonspeech element can justify limitations of First Amendment freedoms," the Court ruled, in a decision from which only Justice Douglas dissented. *O'Brien*'s patriotic fervor alarmed civil libertarians, who realized that almost any act of "speech" could be said to include a "nonspeech" element.

In a contrasting decision, *Tinker* v. *Des Moines* (1969), the Court moved to protect symbolic speech, overturning the Des Moines School District's decision to suspend students who wore black armbands protesting the War. Justice Black dissented on the ground that the students were engaged in action, not speech. In his *Tinker* dissent, Black seemed guided by the fears of growing lawlessness that had first surfaced five years earlier with the sit-in cases, as he painted a dark picture of judicially sanctioned anarchy.

I repeat that if the time has come when pupils . . . can defy and flout orders of school officials to keep their minds on their own schoolwork, it is the beginning of a new revolutionary era of permissiveness in this country fostered by the judiciary . . . [S]tudents all over the land are already running loose, conducting break-ins, sit-ins, lie-ins, and smash-ins. Many of these student groups, as is all too familiar to all who read the newspapers and watch the television news programs, have already engaged in rioting, property seizures, and destruction.

The speech-action distinction to which Black clung in *Tinker* received perhaps its greatest blow in the 1971 case *Cohen* v. *California*. In *Cohen*, the Court in a 5–4 decision overturned the breach-of-peace conviction of a man who had walked through a Los Angeles courthouse wearing a jacket emblazoned with the words "Fuck the Draft." The dissenters, including Black, declared that "Cohen's absurd and immature antic . . . was mainly conduct and little speech." In fact, "speech" and "action" were inextricably intertwined in Cohen's behavior. *O'Brien, Tinker,* and *Cohen* all signaled that First Amendment jurisprudence had not yet managed to acknowledge that symbolic speech undermined the distinction between speech and action.

The Right to Privacy

The Warren Court expanded constitutional freedoms both in the public sphere and in the most private realms of decisions about sexuality and birth control. The Court recognized that a zone of privacy immune from intrusion by government was a necessary precondition for individual self-realization and for a democratic society. The dystopias of *1984* and *Brave New World* suggest what society might be like if privacy and sexuality were sacrificed to the greater good of the state; democracy requires that citizens retain a measure of autonomy not only in public speech but also in the private choices they make about their own bodies.

In *Griswold* v. *Connecticut* (1965), one of the Warren Court's most controversial and far-reaching decisions, the Court first recognized a constitutional right to privacy, barring the state of Connecticut from enforcing its statute forbidding use of contraceptives by married couples.

By the time the Connecticut birth control law was challenged, public attitudes toward contraception had undergone a 180-

degree change from early in the twentieth century, when Margaret Sanger had begun her battle against laws barring doctors from offering birth control advice. At that time, the federal Comstock Law forbade the mailing, interstate transportation, and importation of contraceptive materials and information; twenty-two states also had "little Comstock laws," of which the most restrictive was Connecticut's absolute ban on the "use" of birth control devices.

Through the 1920s, Sanger scored very few successes in her efforts to appeal to courts to relax the severity of these laws. But the educational efforts of the Planned Parenthood Federation, supported by First Lady Eleanor Roosevelt, brought the movement to "a new phase" during the 1940s "in which birth control began to enjoy substantial social and official acceptance." Yet political stalemate or inertia kept most of the old anti–birth control laws on the books, so that they continued to threaten law-abiding citizens, even though prosecutors rarely enforced them. And in the way that all laws are symbolic of community values, they conveyed a message about sexuality and the legitimacy of governmental intrusion into the most intimate realms.

By the time *Griswold* v. *Connecticut* was decided, then, a substantial consensus had emerged on the desirability of family planning through contraception. Even Justice Stewart, who believed Connecticut's anti–birth control statute should be upheld, called it an "uncommonly silly law." The question to be decided in *Griswold* was whether there was a constitutional basis for striking down such laws. Writing the opinion of the Court, Justice Douglas found that the Connecticut law unconstitutionally interfered with "notions of privacy surrounding the marriage relationship." The law intruded into "an intimate relation of husband and wife and their physician's role in . . . that relation."

But where did the Constitution provide for any right to privacy? Various interpretations of the Fourth and Fifth Amendments by the Court, Douglas declared, have created "penumbral rights of 'privacy and repose.' " A "zone of privacy [has been] created by several fundamental constitutional guarantees." Cases interpreting these specific provisions "suggest that specific guarantees in the Bill of Rights have penumbras, formed by emanations from those guarantees that help give them life and substance."

As if Douglas's talk of "penumbras" and "emanations" were not provocative enough, Justice Goldberg (with the support of Chief Justice Warren and Justice Brennan) added an even more controversial note to the question of how to locate the right to privacy in the text of the Constitution. He invoked the long-dormant Ninth Amendment, which states that "[t]he enumeration in the Constitution, of certain rights, shall not be construed to deny or disparage others retained by the people." Goldberg acknowledged that the amendment had played no role in almost two hundred years of constitutional history. Its words had always been thought of as no more than what Justice Stone, referring to similar words in the Tenth Amendment, had dismissed as a "truism that all is retained which has not been surrendered."

All of these intellectual gymnastics, it should be recognized, were devoted to avoiding Justice Harlan's more straightforward approach of holding that the "right to privacy" was included within the Fourteenth Amendment's Due Process Clause. For the liberal justices, however, who had spent years criticizing the *Lochner* Court for supposedly illegitimately changing from a "procedural" to a "substantive" interpretation of due process, nothing could have been worse than deriving a right to privacy from the Due Process Clause.

Though it is beyond the chronological scope of this book, we should note here that *Griswold* v. *Connecticut* became the leading precedent for the Court's extension of the right to privacy to include a woman's right to an abortion in *Roe* v. *Wade* (1973), the most controversial Supreme Court decision in many years. Until that moment, the result in *Griswold* was quite popular, even if its methodology was widely criticized within the legal profession.

Justice Black's dissent in *Griswold* was a direct criticism of its methodology. One year after the first sit-in cases split the new liberal majority, *Griswold* represented another major step in Black's alienation from his former allies. Stating that the Connecticut law "is every bit as offensive to me as it is" to the majority, Black nevertheless denied "that the evil qualities they see in the law make it unconstitutional . . . I like my privacy as well as the next one," Black continued, "but I am nevertheless compelled to admit that government has a right to invade it unless prohibited by some specific constitutional provision." Both the Ninth Amendment grounds of Justice Goldberg and the due process grounds of Justice Harlan "turn out to be the same thing—merely using different words to claim for this Court and the federal judiciary power to invalidate any legislative act which the judges find irrational, unreasonable or offensive."

Black here reiterated a view that he had expressed as long ago as *Adamson* v. *California* (1947), when, as we saw in Chapter 5, he first crossed swords with Justice Frankfurter's effort to base due process on ideas of fundamental fairness in criminal procedure. Anything short of total incorporation of the Bill of Rights into the Due Process Clause Black then denounced as a subjective appeal to "natural law." Yet, on the basis of a controversial reading of the original intent of the Framers of the Fourteenth Amendment that to some critics seemed equally arbitrary, Black maintained that history justified total incorporation.

Black's rigid originalism and textualism reduced every complex interpretative argument to a one-dimensional test: whether an interpretation was "objective" or "subjective." Here he was echoing arguments developed by Protestant fundamentalist ministers, arguments that he had surely heard in church in his youth. Southern evangelicals had traditionally opposed all biblical interpretation and insisted on finding a "plain meaning" in the biblical text. We should recall that Black referred to the Constitution as "my legal bible" and "cherish[ed] every word of it, from the first to the last . . . personally deplor[ing] even the slightest deviation from its least important commands." Black followed his ancestors in seeking the original meaning of their sacred texts and refusing to acknowledge that those texts might change with changing times.

Using the twin criteria of textual literalism and historical originalism, Black righteously claimed objectivity for his own dogmatic readings of the Constitution; yet his position enmeshed him in contradiction. Though he was ardently opposed to the idea of a "living Constitution," he had been able to conclude that the Equal Protection Clause originally barred racial segregation as well as unequal apportionment in both houses of state legislatures, propositions that could only be defended on the basis of a dynamic view of evolving constitutional meaning.

As Black grew older and more disillusioned with the freewheeling interpretative style of his former allies, he became even more rigid in his denunciation of constitutional interpretation designed "to bring [the Constitution] into harmony with the times." In another privacy case, he took this opposition to the point of absurdity.

Katz v. *United States* (1967) involved wiretapping by FBI agents who had attached an electronic listening and recording device to the outside of a public telephone booth from which the defendant had placed his calls. The government insisted that unless there was a trespass onto the defendant's own property there could be no "unreasonable search and seizure" in violation of the Fourth Amendment. Rejecting this view, Justice Stewart held that the Amendment was meant to protect not the defendant's property but, rather, his privacy.

Justice Black was the lone dissenter. He wrote: "A conversation overheard by eavesdropping, whether by plain snooping or wiretapping, is not tangible and, under the normally accepted meanings of the words, can neither be searched nor seized." Black's rigid literalism was not far from Chief Justice Taft's original refusal in *Olmstead* v. *United States* (1928) to include wiretapping under the Fourth Amendment because the Framers could not have intended to cover this unknown technology by the protection against unreasonable searches and seizures. Justice Brandeis had the better of the argument in dissent, emphasizing that the Fourth Amendment's underlying principle of protecting privacy from intrusions by the state would apply even to previously unknown technology.

Though the Douglas and Goldberg opinions in *Griswold* v. *Connecticut* were stated in more untraditional language, they were making the same point as Brandeis made in *Olmstead*. Courts frequently search for the underlying principle of a rule before deciding whether to apply it to new situations. And not infrequently, when they are asked to extend a rule to a new situation, they find support for the extension in the fact that many different existing rules are supported by the same underlying principle.

This was what Justice Douglas meant when he found converging "penumbras" and "emanations" of the right to privacy in various constitutional rules such as the Fourth and Fifth Amendments. Even Justice Goldberg's invocation of the Ninth Amendment was more traditional in its methodology than has often been acknowledged. "I [do not] mean to state that the Ninth Amendment constitutes an independent source of rights," Goldberg emphasized, but, rather, that it "shows a belief of the Constitution's authors that fundamental rights exist that are not expressly enumerated in the first eight amendments and an intent that the list of rights included there not be deemed exhaustive."

Like its protection of artistic expression, the Court's privacy decisions were based on an understanding of the multiple layers of human personality and self-expression that constitute a thriving democratic culture. The protection of human sexuality independent of procreation was the foundation of *Griswold*; protection of such spontaneous intimate relationships lies at the basis of an autonomous democratic culture.

VII

Conclusion

As the Warren Court gradually fades from collective memory and becomes "history," it is all the more important to see it in historical perspective, free, as much as possible, of the slogans and abstractions of contemporary constitutional debate. Today's popular discourse frequently depicts the Warren Court disapprovingly as a model of judicial activism; on the other side of the coin, the Court's champions will point out that it was not so "activist" after all, or that the Burger or Rehnquist Court has really been more activist. But discussions of the Warren Court in terms of the judicial activism/restraint dichotomy can be misleading. Such accounts suppose that there is some "objective" historical norm or baseline of judicial review as it has been practiced over more than two hundred years of constitutional history. Any textured consideration of American constitutional history, however, would demonstrate that there has never been a reliable standard of judicial restraint in Supreme Court jurisprudence. Rather, the boundaries of acceptable judicial review have always been contested and have fluctuated in response to changing historical circumstances.

During the 1980s, Attorney General Edwin Meese provoked a decade of academic debate by proposing "original intent" as the historical baseline by which to judge—and ultimately, he hoped, to discredit—the performance of the Warren Court. The responses to Meese overwhelmingly demonstrated the intellectual inadequacy of any single formula, whether it appealed to original intent or to the "plain meaning" of the constitutional text, to produce an "objective" standard for the Supreme Court's role in constitutional interpretation. Justice Brennan called Meese's originalism "arrogance cloaked as humility." "It is arrogant to pretend from our vantage point we can gauge accurately the intent of the Framers on application of principle to specific, contemporary sources," Brennan wrote.

Any standard purporting to set an acceptable level of "activism" for the Supreme Court must rely on a particular prior conception of the role of the Constitution and the Supreme Court in American life. The liberal majority that made the Warren Court distinctive had its own inspiring vision of that role.

Each of the seven liberal justices of the Warren Court was a powerful representative of the spirit of American progressive politics as it had developed since the beginning of the twentieth century. Each saw himself as part of one of the strands of American liberalism forged by the heirs of Theodore Roosevelt, Woodrow Wilson, and especially Franklin Roosevelt. All but Warren were closely connected by position or sentiment with Roosevelt's New Deal. For each of the justices other than Warren, FDR's New Deal represented the highest attainment of American liberalism. Warren himself was a distinct political type, a Western Progressive Republican, a California Republican, who was often accused of harboring liberal Democratic sentiments.

Our focus on the Warren Court liberals should also remind us that the two most important Warren Court conservatives, Stewart and Harlan, were appointed at a time when liberal Eastern Republicans (from the Eisenhower or, later, Rockefeller wings) were in control of the party. There was much more agreement between them and the Warren Court liberals than would be true of Republican appointees today.

In addition to their general politics, the Warren Court liberals shared a number of beliefs about the place of law in modern American society that were part of the American progressive heritage. The Warren Court was an expression of both the spirit and the contradictions of liberal American jurisprudence.

The legal consciousness of the Warren Court liberals had been shaped by the struggle between Progressivism and the *Lochner* Court, which culminated in the New Deal triumph after 1937. At the core of that struggle was the question of the constitutional legitimacy of the federal government's regulation of the economy. Contradictory lessons emerged from that struggle. The split between Frankfurter and Black, as we have seen, turned on a disagreement over the proper lessons about judicial review to be learned from the *Lochner* era.

Despite the varying origins of their political progressivism, the Warren Court liberals shared a vision of law that the Legal Realists of the 1920s and 1930s had incorporated into New Deal legal consciousness. Justice Brennan summarized that view: "The genius of the Constitution," he wrote, "rests not in any static meaning it might have had in a world that is dead and gone, but in the adaptability of its great principles to cope with current problems and current needs." Except for Justice Black, all of the other liberal justices would have wholeheartedly agreed with Brennan's statement. And even Black, who as he grew older went out of his way to denounce any notion of a "living" Constitution, was less dogmatic about changing constitutional meanings earlier in his career.

Yet the social reformers' conception of law as a malleable instrument of social policy often clashed with the Progressive critique of the *Lochner* Court's failure to defer to legislative judgment. For those like Justice Frankfurter who believed that avoiding the errors of the *Lochner* era required almost complete deference to the legislature, the decision in *Brown* v. *Board of Education* shattered any easy identification of liberalism with judicial restraint. Frankfurter's intellectual disciples would be obsessed with reconciling *Brown* with their criticism of *Lochner*.

What did the Warren Court stand for? Like no other Court before or since, it stood for an expansive conception of the democratic way of life as the foundational ideal of constitutional interpretation. Reacting to the "neutral principles" school of legal thought associated with Frankfurter, the Warren Court liberals understood that it was impossible not to incorporate one's deepest values into constitutional interpretation. In his later years, as we have seen, Justice Brennan insisted that a "balance of reason and passion" provided the best antidote to a kind of "abstract rationality" that loses touch with "the pulse of life beneath the official version of events."

The Warren Court's inclusive idea of democracy was built on the revival of the Equal Protection Clause in *Brown*. It then spread beyond race cases to cover other outsiders in American society: religious minorities, political radicals, aliens, ethnic minorities, prisoners, and criminal defendants.

Justice Brennan frequently justified Warren Court decisions expanding constitutional rights by pointing to their contribution to protecting "human dignity." The focus of these decisions was, as Brennan put it, on "whether individual dignity has been honored, whether the worth of an individual has been acknowledged." It should be emphasized again that the Warren Court thought of these "rights" decisions as integral to democracy, not as a departure from the normal democratic process. Nor did Brennan find any contradiction between protecting "essential human dignity" and endorsing a changing Constitution whose "genius" lay "in the adaptability of its great principles to cope with current problems and current needs."

Appendix
Composition of the Warren Court 1953–69

1953

Liberals	Conservatives
Earl Warren (1953–69)	Stanley F. Reed (1938–57)
Hugo L. Black (1937–71)	Felix Frankfurter (1939–62)
William O. Douglas (1939–75)	Robert H. Jackson (1941–54)
	Harold H. Burton (1945–58)
	Tom C. Clark (1949–67)
	Sherman Minton (1949–56)

1956

Liberals	Conservatives
Earl Warren (1953–69)	Stanley F. Reed (1938–57)
Hugo L. Black (1937–71)	Felix Frankfurter (1939–62)
William O. Douglas (1939–75)	Harold H. Burton (1945–58)
William J. Brennan, Jr. (1956–90)	Tom C. Clark (1949–67)
	John Marshall Harlan (1955–71)

1962

Liberals	Conservatives
Earl Warren (1953–69)	Tom C. Clark (1949–67)
Hugo L. Black (1937–71)	John Marshall Harlan (1955–71)
William O. Douglas (1939–75)	Potter Stewart (1958–81)
William J. Brennan, Jr. (1956–90)	Byron R. White (1962–93)
Arthur J. Goldberg (1962–65)	

1969

Liberals	Conservatives
Earl Warren (1953–69)	John Marshall Harlan (1955–71)
Hugo L. Black (1937–71)	Potter Stewart (1958–81)
William O. Douglas (1939–75)	Byron R. White (1962–93)
William J. Brennan, Jr. (1956–90)	
Abe Fortas (1965–69)	
Thurgood Marshall (1967–91)	

Bibliography

On Justice Black

Ball, Howard. *Hugo Black: Cold Steel Warrior*. New York: Oxford University Press, 1996.

———. *Of Power and Right: Hugo Black, William O. Douglas, and America's Constitutional Revolution*. New York: Oxford University Press, 1992.

Black, Hugo L. *A Constitutional Faith*. New York: Knopf, 1968.

Black, Hugo L., and Elizabeth Black. *Mr. Justice and Mrs. Black: Memoirs*. New York: Random House, 1986.

Dunne, Gerald T. *Hugo Black and the Judicial Revolution*. New York: Simon & Schuster, 1977.

Freyer, Tony. *Hugo L. Black and the Dilemma of American Liberalism*. Glenview, Ill.: Scott, Foresman/Little, Brown, 1990.

Freyer, Tony, ed. *Justice Hugo Black and Modern America*. Tuscaloosa, Ala.: University of Alabama Press, 1990.

Hockett, Jeffrey D. *New Deal Justice: The Constitutional Jurisprudence of Hugo L. Black, Felix Frankfurter, and Robert H. Jackson*. Lanham, Md.: Rowman & Littlefield Publishers, 1996.

Newman, Roger K. *Hugo Black: A Biography*. New York: Pantheon Books, 1994.

Silverstein, Mark. *Constitutional Faiths: Felix Frankfurter, Hugo Black, and the Process of Judicial Decision Making*. Ithaca, N.Y.: Cornell University Press, 1984.

Simon, James F. *The Antagonists: Hugo Black, Felix Frankfurter and Civil Liberties in Modern America*. New York: Simon & Schuster, 1989.

Yarbrough, Tinsley E. *Mr. Justice Black and His Critics*. Durham, N.C.: Duke University Press, 1988.

On Justice Brennan

Clark, Hunter R. *Justice Brennan: The Great Conciliator*. New York: Carol Publishing Group, 1995.

Eisler, Kim Isaac. *A Justice for All: William J. Brennan, Jr., and the Decisions That Transformed America*. New York: Simon & Schuster, 1993.

Rosenkranz, E. Joshua, and Bernard Schwartz, eds. *Reason and Passion: Justice Brennan's Enduring Influence*. New York: Norton, 1997.

On Justice Clark

Beeman, Mary Purser. *New Deal Justice: Tom Clark and the Warren Court, 1953–1967*. Ann Arbor: University of Michigan Press, 1993.

On Justice Douglas

Ball, Howard. *Of Power and Right: Hugo Black, William O. Douglas, and America's Constitutional Revolution*. New York: Oxford University Press, 1992.

Countryman, Vern. *The Judicial Record of Justice William O. Douglas*. Cambridge: Harvard University Press, 1974.

Douglas, William O. *Go East, Young Man: The Early Years: The Autobiography of William O. Douglas*. New York: Random House, 1974.

———. *The Court Years: The Autobiography of William O. Douglas*. New York: Random House, 1980.

Simon, James F. *Independent Journey: The Life of William O. Douglas*. New York: Harper & Row, 1980.

Wasby, Stephen L., ed. *"He Shall Not Pass This Way Again": The Legacy of Justice William O. Douglas*. Pittsburgh: University of Pittsburgh Press, 1990.

On Justice Fortas

Kalman, Laura. *Abe Fortas: A Biography*. New Haven: Yale University Press, 1990.

On Justice Frankfurter

Baker, Leonard. *Brandeis and Frankfurter: A Dual Biography*. New York: Harper & Row, 1984.

Baker, Liva. *Felix Frankfurter.* New York: Coward-McCann, 1969.

Burt, Robert. *Two Jewish Justices: Outcasts in the Promised Land.* Berkeley: University of California Press, 1988.

Hirsch, Harry N. *The Enigma of Felix Frankfurter.* New York: Basic Books, 1981.

Hockett, Jeffrey D. *New Deal Justice: The Constitutional Jurisprudence of Hugo L. Black, Felix Frankfurter, and Robert H. Jackson.* Lanham, Md.: Rowman & Littlefield Publishers, 1996.

Kurland, Philip B. *Mr. Justice Frankfurter and the Constitution.* Chicago: University of Chicago Press, 1971.

Parrish, Michael E. *Felix Frankfurter and His Time: The Reform Years.* New York: Free Press; London: Collier Macmillan, 1982.

Silverstein, Mark. *Constitutional Faiths: Felix Frankfurter, Hugo Black, and the Process of Judicial Decision Making.* Ithaca, N.Y.: Cornell University Press, 1984.

Simon, James F. *The Antagonists: Hugo Black, Felix Frankfurter and Civil Liberties in Modern America.* New York: Simon & Schuster, 1989.

Urofsky, Melvin I. *Felix Frankfurter: Judicial Restraint and Individual Liberties.* Boston: Twayne, 1991.

On Justice Goldberg

Stebenne, David. *Arthur J. Goldberg: New Deal Liberal.* New York: Oxford University Press, 1996.

On Justice Harlan

Yarbrough, Tinsley E. *John Marshall Harlan: Great Dissenter of the Warren Court.* New York: Oxford University Press, 1992.

On Justice Marshall

Rowan, Carl Thomas. *Dream Makers, Dream Breakers: The World of Justice Thurgood Marshall.* Boston: Little, Brown, 1993.

Tushnet, Mark V. *Making Civil Rights Law: Thurgood Marshall and the Supreme Court, 1936–1961.* New York: Oxford University Press, 1994.

———. *Making Constitutional Law: Thurgood Marshall and the Supreme Court, 1961–1991.* New York: Oxford University Press, 1997.

On Justice Warren

Cray, Ed. *Chief Justice: A Biography of Earl Warren*. New York: Simon & Schuster, 1997.

Schwartz, Bernard. *Super Chief: Earl Warren and His Supreme Court*. New York: New York University Press, 1983.

Warren, Earl. *The Memoirs of Earl Warren*. Garden City, N.Y.: Doubleday, 1977.

White, G. Edward. *Earl Warren: A Public Life*. New York: Oxford University Press, 1982.

On Justice White

University of Colorado Law Review 58 (1987). [Special issue devoted to Justice White.]

On the Warren Court

Bickel, Alexander M. *Politics and the Warren Court*. New York: Harper & Row, 1965.

———. *The Supreme Court and the Idea of Progress*. New Haven: Yale University Press, 1978.

Cox, Archibald. *The Warren Court: Constitutional Decision as an Instrument of Reform*. Cambridge: Harvard University Press, 1968.

Rotunda, Ronald D. *Six Justices on Civil Rights*. New York: Oceana Publications, 1983. [Includes essays on Black, Douglas, and Frankfurter.]

Schwartz, Bernard, ed. *The Warren Court: A Retrospective*. New York: Oxford University Press, 1996.

Tushnet, Mark, ed. *The Warren Court in Historical and Political Perspective*. Charlottesville: University of Virginia Press, 1993.

On Criminal Law and Due Process

Cortner, Richard C. *The Supreme Court and the Second Bill of Rights: The Fourteenth Amendment and the Nationalization of Civil Liberties*. Madison: University of Wisconsin Press, 1981.

Kamisar, Yale. *Police Interrogation and Confessions*. Ann Arbor: University of Michigan Press, 1980.

Lewis, Anthony. *Gideon's Trumpet*. New York: Random House, 1964.

Schwartz, Bernard. *The Fourteenth Amendment.* New York: New York University Press, 1970.

Stephens, Otis H. *The Supreme Court and Confessions of Guilt.* Knoxville: University of Tennessee Press, 1973.

On Desegregation and Civil Rights

Abraham, Henry Julian. *Freedom and the Court: Civil Rights and Liberties in the United States.* 6th ed. New York: Oxford University Press, 1994.

Bickel, Alexander M. "The Original Understanding and the Segregation Decision." *Harvard Law Review* 69 (1955): 1–65.

Branch, Taylor. *Parting the Waters: America in the King Years 1954–1963.* New York: Simon & Schuster, 1988.

Freyer, Tony. *The Little Rock Crisis.* Westport, Conn.: Greenwood Press, 1984.

Kluger, Richard. *Simple Justice.* New York: Knopf, 1976.

Tushnet, Mark. *The NAACP's Legal Strategy Against Segregated Education, 1925–1950.* Chapel Hill: University of North Carolina Press, 1987.

On the First Amendment

Kalven, Harry. *A Worthy Tradition: Freedom of Speech in America.* New York: Harper & Row, 1988.

Lewis, Anthony. *Make No Law: The Sullivan Case and the First Amendment.* New York: Random House, 1991.

Rabban, David M. *Free Speech in Its Forgotten Years.* Cambridge: Cambridge University Press, 1997.

———. "The Emergence of Modern First Amendment Doctrine." *University of Chicago Law Review* 50 (1983): 1205.

Schwartz, Bernard. *Freedom of the Press.* New York: Facts on File, 1992.

On McCarthyism

Belknap, Michael R. *Cold War Political Justice: The Smith Act, the Communist Party, and American Civil Liberties.* Westport, Conn.: Greenwood Press, 1977.

Fried, Richard M. *Nightmare in Red: The McCarthy Era in Perspective.* New York: Oxford University Press, 1990.

Heale, M. J. *American Anticommunism: Combating the Enemy Within, 1830–1970*. Baltimore: Johns Hopkins University Press, 1990.
Murphy, Paul L. *The Constitution in Crisis Times, 1918–1969*. New York: Harper & Row, 1972.

On Reapportionment

McKay, Robert B. *Reapportionment: The Law and Politics of Equal Representation*. New York: The Twentieth Century Fund, 1965.

Index